Enriching Faith

LESSONS AND ACTIVITIES ON MARY

MARY KATHLEEN GLAVICH, SND

I0806877

TWENTY-THIRD PUBLICATIONS
twentythirdpublications.com

TWENTY-THIRD PUBLICATIONS
One Montauk Avenue, Suite 200
New London, CT 06320
(860) 437-3012 or (800) 321-0411
www.twentythirdpublications.com

Copyright © 2016 Mary Kathleen Glavich, SND.
Permission is given to reproduce the activity pages in this book as needed for non-commercial use in schools and parish religious education programs. Otherwise, no part of this publication may be reproduced in any manner without prior written permission of the publisher. Write to the Permissions Editor.

ISBN: 978-1-62785-145-9
Library of Congress Control Number: 2015957201
Printed in the U.S.A.

A division of Bayard, Inc.

CONTENTS

INTRODUCTION

One thing that distinguishes Catholics is our devotion to the Blessed Virgin Mary, the woman God chose to be the mother of his Son. We admire Mary as a faithful handmaid of the Lord, strive to imitate her as the first and best disciple, and love her as our heavenly mother. Our Lady has inspired such devotion in artists and writers that she appears in more artwork and literature than any other woman. Cathedrals are built in her honor, and hymns are composed about her.

We are greatly indebted to Mary because, through her, Jesus came into the world and won eternal life back for us. As Blessed Mother Teresa of Calcutta succinctly said, "No Mary. No Jesus." Mary's role as mother of the Savior involved such suffering that we call her Queen of Martyrs. Her work for us continues. Mary is our powerful intercessor. Several times she has visited earth and invited us to come to her for help. She also urged us to pray and do penance. The mother of Jesus loves and cares for us, who are Jesus' brothers and sisters. St. Anselm commented, "There is never enough said or written about Mary."

Sadly, not everyone understands the Virgin Mary. Some regard her as a goddess, too sublime to be approached or imitated. Others ignore our Blessed Mother, saying that they prefer to go directly to God. Many people confuse the doctrine of the Immaculate Conception with the virgin birth. The lessons in this book clarify for children what the church teaches about Mary. They also invite children to reflect upon who Mary is for them. They present Mary's life as revealed in Scripture and church doctrine. In addition, they introduce children to the Marian prayers and devotions that the church encourages us to practice. These have developed over the centuries to honor Our Lady and express our love. When we show devotion to Mary, we please her Son. When we model our lives on hers, we are more assured of joining her and Jesus in heaven.

The Book

For each of the thirty-two lessons in this book, a one-page plan is provided with one focused objective. Catechist Notes offer background on the topic and also suggest ideas for the lesson. Materials required for the lesson are listed. The steps for developing the topic are few and simple. They engage the children, draw on their experiences, and vary from lesson to lesson. Each lesson is accompanied by an Activity Sheet to be duplicated for the children. These sheets develop or reinforce the lessons in a variety of ways, such as prayer services, plays, art projects, and paper and pencil activities. A brief prayer concludes each lesson.

By supplementing regular religion lessons with the lessons in this book, teachers, catechists, and parents will help to plant a love for the Blessed Virgin Mary in the hearts of children,

1 MARY OF NAZARETH: WOMAN FROM GALILEE

Objective

The children will become familiar with Mary's hometown and culture.

Catechist Notes

Mary was a Jew who lived in Israel some two thousand years ago. Acquainting your children with what Mary's life was like will enable them to know her and her Son better. It will also help them to understand the gospels. You might dress as Mary and let the children interview you about life in Nazareth; or prepare a friend to be Mary, and you ask her questions.

Materials

- ☐ A map or globe
- ☐ A loaf of store-bought bread
- ☐ Copies of Activity Sheet 1

Activity

❶ Explain that Mary lived in Nazareth in what is now the Middle Eastern country of Israel. Help a child locate Israel on a map or globe.

❷ Inform the children that church tradition tells us that Mary's parents (Jesus' grandparents) were Joachim and Anne. We honor them as saints and celebrate their feast day on July 26.

❸ Lead the children to realize how different Mary's life was from ours.

- How long ago did Mary live? (about two thousand years ago)
- What wasn't invented yet?
- The church wasn't established. Mary was Jewish.
- [Show the bread.] Here is one way Mary's life was different. We buy our bread. Mary ground grain and baked bread for her family. Maybe she helped harvest the grain. Most of the people in Nazareth were farmers.

❹ Distribute Activity Sheet 1. Ask the following questions to introduce each fact on it. After each question is answered, have a child read the corresponding fact on the sheet.

1. How many people are in your town or city? (thousands)

2. When did you learn to read and write? (starting at age five)

3. How many rooms does your house have? (Answers will vary.)

4. How do you light your house? (lights and lamps powered by electricity)

5. How many meals do you eat a day? (three)

6. What foods do you mainly eat? (Answers will vary.)

7. How often does your family shop for food? (Answers will vary.)

8. Where do you get your drinking water? (from the tap or a bottle)

9. How are clothes washed at home? (in a machine)

10. What do women wear today? (dresses, slacks, blouses, skirts)

11. At what age do girls today get married? (eighteen and above)

12. What day do we call the Lord's Day? (Sunday)

13. How do we observe the Lord's Day? (rest, celebrate the Eucharist)

14. Where is the center of our Catholic faith located? (Rome)

15. What kind of government does our country have? (democratic; it is a free country.)

Prayer

Jesus, help me be the best I can be in my time and place, like your mother was in hers.

A First-Century Jewish Woman

COMPARE YOUR LIFE TO MARY'S LIFE.

1 Mary lived in Nazareth, a village of about two hundred people, and many of them were related. Nazareth was in the province of Galilee, which is in northern Israel.

2 Girls didn't go to school, so Mary probably couldn't read or write. A woman could not inherit if there was a man in the family. They could not be a witness in court or speak in the synagogue, the house of prayer.

3 Mary lived in a one-room house of stone that had a dirt floor and one small window. When it was hot, she slept on the flat roof.

4 Mary used oil lamps to light her house. People went to bed as soon as it got dark.

5 Mary ate breakfast and then had a larger meal in the evening.

6 Mary ate cheese, eggs, fish, dates, grapes, figs, olives, and bread. Meat was seldom eaten. Because there were no spoons or forks, Mary used her fingers or dipped bread into a common bowl of stew or soup.

7 Because there were no refrigerators, Mary shopped at the market every day.

8 To provide water for her family, every day Mary went to the well, where she met the other village women.

9 Mary washed clothes by hand.

10 Mary wore a long dress and a veil. She spun thread, wove cloth, and then made her family's clothes.

11 Jewish girls could marry at age twelve.

12 For Jewish people, the Lord's Day, or the Sabbath, was Saturday.

13 Mary observed the Sabbath by obeying strict rules, such as not sewing, lighting a fire, tying a rope, or walking more than a certain short distance.

14 The center of the Jewish religion was Jerusalem, the site of the temple, the only place where sacrifices were offered.

15 Israel, or Palestine, as it was then known, was controlled by the Romans, who charged high taxes and oppressed the people.

2 IMMACULATE CONCEPTION: MARY MOST PURE

Objective love that will last a lifetime.
The children will learn that Mary was born without sin and lived a life of holiness.

Catechist Notes

In his poem "The Virgin," William Wordsworth describes Mary as "our tainted nature's solitary boast." The dogma of the Immaculate Conception, declared by Pope Pius IX in 1854, affirms these words. Because Mary is the Mother of God, she was free from original sin through her Son's merits in advance. Also, because Mary was full of grace and not weakened by original sin, she led a sinless life. This lesson will forestall the misconception that the Immaculate Conception refers to the virginal conception of Jesus.

Materials

- ☐ *Immaculate Conception* written on the board or on poster paper
- ☐ A glass of water
- ☐ Pens or pencils
- ☐ Copies of Activity Sheet 2

Activity

1. Show the glass of water and develop the meaning of "immaculate."
   - Some people keep water in purifiers. Why? (to strain out anything that makes the water impure, or not completely water)
   - In stores, you see labels like "100% pure orange juice" or "pure prune juice." Nothing is mixed in with the juice.
   - Another word for pure is "immaculate." What would an immaculate floor, window, or shirt be like? (spotless, stainless)
   - Conception means the very start of a living being within its mother.

2. Explain the dogma of the Immaculate Conception.
   - God preserved Mary from the original sin we all inherited from Adam and Eve. From the first moment of Mary's existence in her mother, she was pure and sinless. We call this the Immaculate Conception.
   - Mary remained filled with grace throughout her life by loving and obeying God. She did not commit sin but lived a life of holiness. She is the model for us of how to live our lives full of divine life and grace.

3. Offer this further information:
   - The feast of the Immaculate Conception is December 8, nine months before we celebrate Mary's birth, on September 8. The feast of the Immaculate Conception is a holy day of obligation.
   - Mary the Immaculate Conception is the patroness of the United States.
   - The National Shrine of the Immaculate Conception is in Washington, DC.
   - Father Jacques Marquette, a missionary and explorer, named the Mississippi River the River of the Immaculate Conception.
   - When Mary appeared to St. Bernadette in Lourdes, France, she identified herself as the Immaculate Conception.

4. Tell the children that God wants us to try to be pure and holy like Mary. Distribute Activity Sheet 2. Direct the children to finish the sentences that give advice for having a pure and holy heart. When they are finished, correct their answers. **Answers:** *1) Hail Marys; 2) tempted; 3) books; 4) movies; 5) friends; 6) Communion; 7) saints; 8) penance.*

Prayer

O Mary, most pure, pray for me that I might have the grace to avoid sin.

A Pure Heart Like Mary's

Mary Immaculate, our mother, would like us to be holy. On each line is advice for creating a pure heart by avoiding sin. Some words are missing. Fill in the blanks by writing the letters that come before the letters below the lines

1 Pray three ____ _____ each night.
I b j m N b s z t

2 When _______, pray a Hail Mary.
u f n q u f e

3 Read good _____.
c p p l t

4 View good ______.
n p w j f t

5 Choose good _______.
g s j f o e t

6 Receive __________.
D p n n v o j p o

7 Learn about the ______.
t b j o u t

1 Celebrate the Sacrament of _______.
q f o b o d f

Trivia Fact!

We celebrate Mary's birthday on September 8, exactly nine months after the feast of the Immaculate Conception, on December 8.

3 ANNUNCIATION: SPOUSE OF THE HOLY SPIRIT

Objective

The children will admire and strive to imitate Mary's openness to God's will.

Catechist Notes

Mary's privileges flow from being Mother of God. Out of all women, Mary of Nazareth was the one God chose to raise his Son as a human being. The feast of the Annunciation of the Lord (March 25) celebrates Mary's agreeing to cooperate with God's plan. Through the Holy Spirit, Jesus was conceived in her, a virgin. The Council of Ephesus in 431 confirmed that Mary was the Mother of God, not only mother of Jesus' human nature. To enhance this lesson, show pictures of the Annunciation.

Materials

- ☐ A BOX CONTAINING A CARD WITH THE WORD *YES*
- ☐ BIBLES
- ☐ PENS OR PENCILS
- ☐ COPIES OF ACTIVITY SHEET 3

Activity

1. Show a box that contains the word Yes. Pose this riddle:
   - In this box is a very important word. The world's salvation depended on it. Guess what it is. [If necessary, give clues: It has three letters. It was Mary's response when God asked her to be his mother.]
   - [Display the word Yes.] Today you will learn about the great day Mary said yes to God.

2. Distribute the Bibles. Help the children locate Luke 1:26–38. Choose a child to read the angel Gabriel's words and a child to read Mary's. They might act out their parts. Tell the rest of the class to read the other parts. Have the passage read. [Or have the children close their eyes and picture the story as you read it.]

3. Discuss Mary's openness to God's will. You might inform the children that under Jewish law unmarried pregnant girls could be stoned to death.
   - Why do you think God chose Mary to be his mother? (She was holy.)
   - How must Mary have felt when she heard the news? (surprised, happy, frightened)
   - Mary was to give birth to Jesus by the Holy Spirit's power. She became pregnant yet remained a virgin, just like light passing through a windowpane doesn't change the windowpane.
   - What other miraculous event did Gabriel tell Mary about? (Elderly Elizabeth was pregnant.)
   - Why did it take courage for Mary to say yes to God's plan? (No one had ever been Mother of God. She didn't know what the child would be like. Joseph would be puzzled and hurt. Mary's parents and neighbors wouldn't understand how she became pregnant. She risked gossip and scorn.)
   - What did Mary call herself? (God's handmaid, servant)
   - What difficult things does God ask you to do?

4. Distribute Activity Sheet 3. Tell the children to see who can fill in the most words related to the Annunciation, using the letters in the word. After a set time, call on children to give answers and explain how they relate to the Annunciation. **Possible answers:** GAbriel, aNgel, Nazareth, SoN, JaCob, DavId, ElizAbeth, Throne, Holy SpIrit, JOseph, haNdmaid or servaNt.

Prayer

Mary, you let God use you in order to save the world. Pray that I may always say yes to God as you did.

The Annunciation of the Lord

Think of words related to the Annunciation story that contain a letter in the word "Annunciation." For each letter, write a word on the line. Be ready to explain why you chose each word.

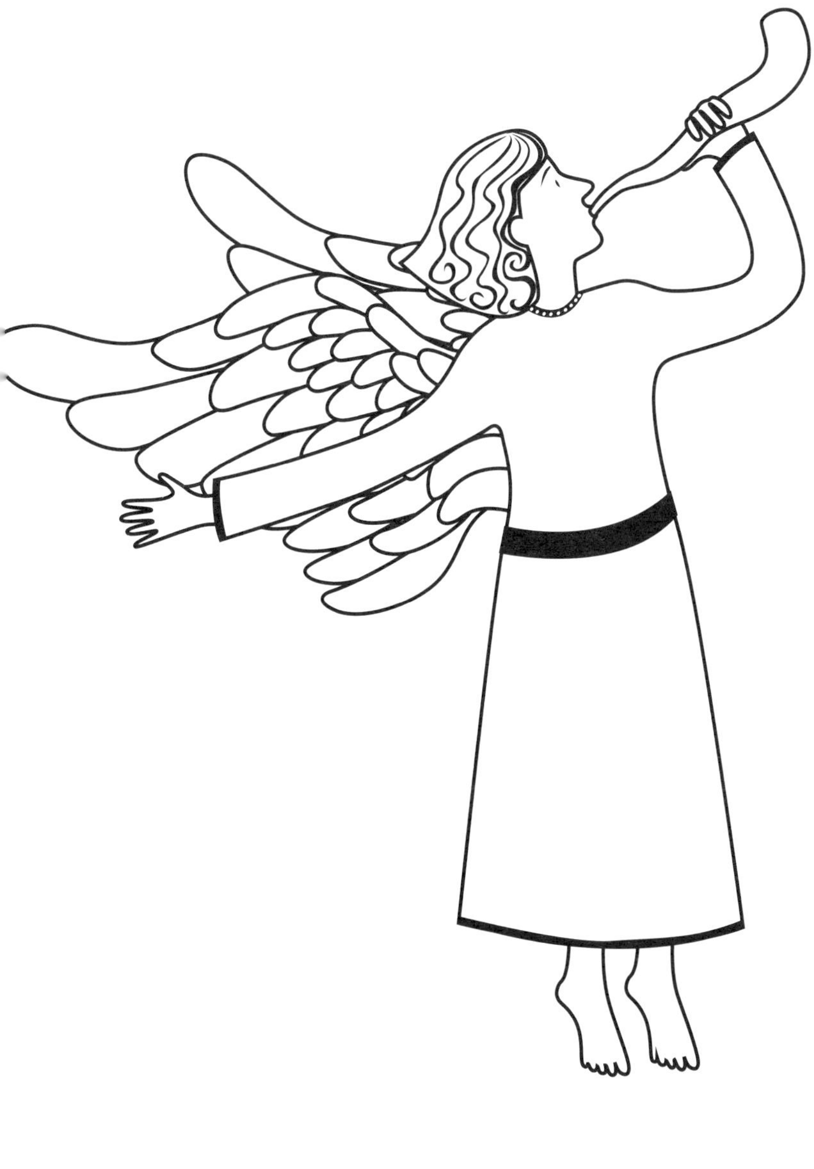

A ____________________

N ____________________

N ____________________

U ____________________

N ____________________

C ____________________

I ____________________

A ____________________

T ____________________

I ____________________

O ____________________

N ____________________

Nothing will be impossible with God.

LUKE 1:38

4 VISITATION: CHRISTBEARER

Objective

The children will realize that Mary showed selfless love in journeying to help Elizabeth.

Catechist Notes

Mary was the first Christopher, or *Christbearer*. St. Catherine of Siena called her the "chariot of fire." Mary, although pregnant, made a perilous journey to help her aged cousin. At Mary's greeting, the baby within Elizabeth, John the Baptist, leapt. Elizabeth recognized that Mary was the Savior's mother. Mary helped with chores and was a companion to Elizabeth, whose husband, Zechariah, was mute. After doing their good deeds, the children might return the footprints for you to display.

Materials

- ☐ Chalk and a board or a felt-tipped pen and poster paper or a whiteboard
- ☐ Crayons or felt-tipped pens
- ☐ Cards with these words: *Home, School, Playground, Neighborhood*
- ☐ Scissors
- ☐ Copies of Activity Sheet 4

Activity

1. Write "Good Samaritan." Ask what it means to call someone a good Samaritan. (The person has helped someone.) Explain:
   - The term comes from a parable Jesus told about a man from Samaria who took care of a man who was beaten and robbed.
   - Why could we call Jesus a good Samaritan? (He helped everyone get to heaven. He cured people.)
   - Today you will see how Mary, his mother, was a good Samaritan.

2. Tell the story of the Visitation. Draw illustrations of the items in parentheses.
   - The angel Gabriel told Mary that her elderly cousin Elizabeth was pregnant. She needed help. Mary had a good excuse not to go to help her. She was pregnant with Jesus. But Mary quickly made the trip.

     The journey was about ninety miles and sometimes uphill *(hill)*. The road was rocky *(rocks on hill)*. The sun was hot *(sun)*. Mary probably walked *(footprints on the hill)*. She wasn't feeling well because she was pregnant. Thieves attacked travelers on that road *(knife)*. When Mary entered the house *(rectangle house)* and greeted Elizabeth, the baby inside Elizabeth leapt. *[Write* John.*]* The Holy Spirit *(dove)* let Elizabeth know that Mary was the Savior's mother, and she cried out, "Blessed are you among women, and blessed is the fruit of your womb." Mary stayed three months and then made the long trip back home.
   - What did Mary probably do to help Elizabeth? (cook for her and her husband, sew baby clothes, wash clothes, fetch water, help deliver the baby)

3. Form groups and give each a card. Ask them to think of ways they can help like Mary in the place named on their cards. After a time, ask the groups to report. Comment:
   - When you do a loving deed for someone, it is as though you are bringing Jesus and his love to them.

4. Distribute Activity Sheet 4. Direct the children to write on each footprint a way they intend to be a good Samaritan, like their mother Mary. Have them color the footprints like their shoes, cut them out, and take them home as reminders.

Prayer

Jesus, you and your mother were quick to help others. Please give me the heart of a good Samaritan too.

A Good Samaritan like Mary

Think of two ways you can be a good Samaritan. Write one way in each footprint and intend to do it. Color the footprints to look like your shoes. Cut them out and keep them at home as reminders.

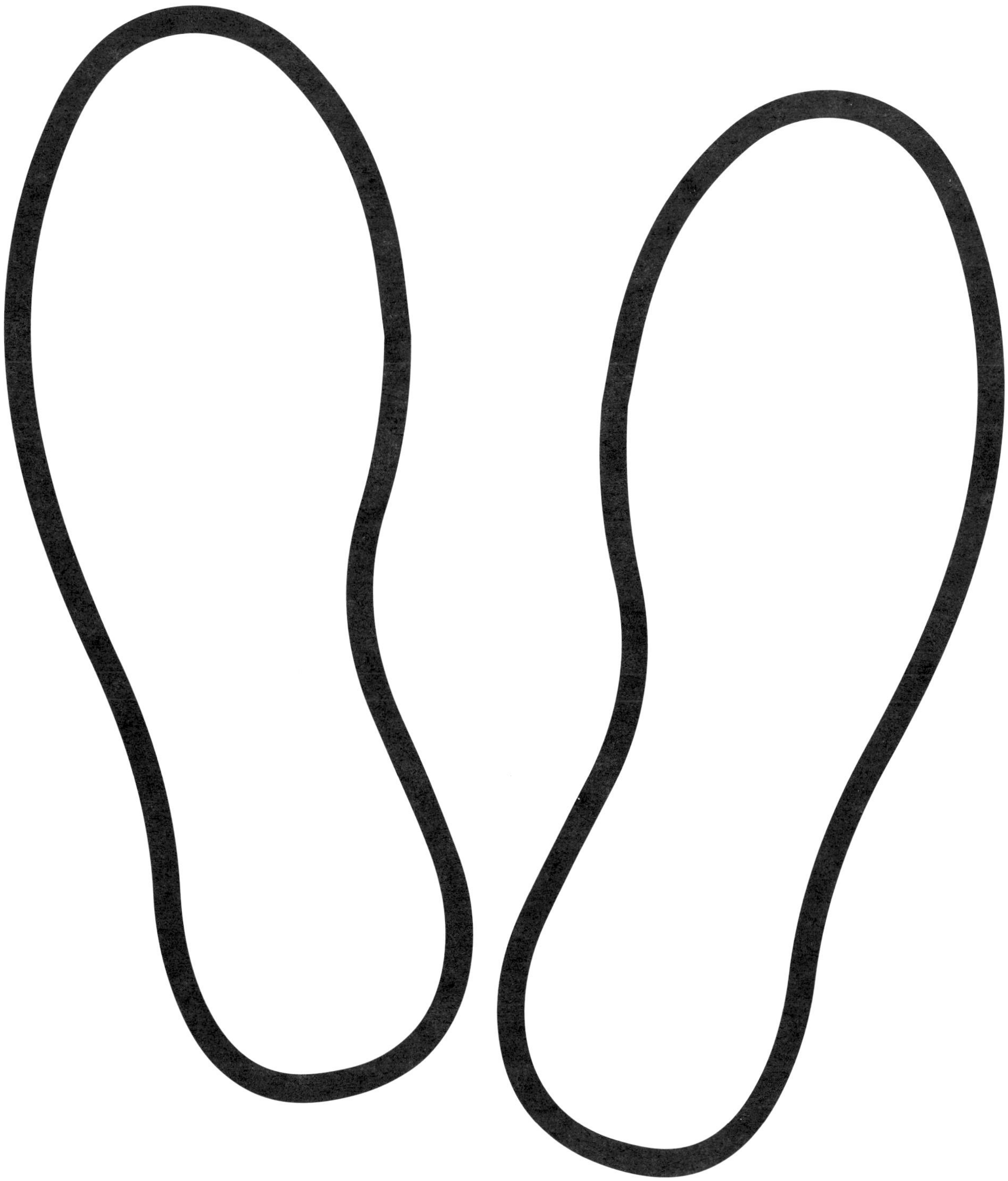

5 MAGNIFICAT: BLESSED VIRGIN

Objective

The children will identify Mary's canticle as a hymn of praise and humble gratitude.

Catechist Notes

The *Magnificat* on Mary's lips at the Visitation weaves together Old Testament themes. In particular, it echoes the canticle of Hannah in 1 Samuel 2:1–10. After years of barrenness, Hannah bore a son, Samuel, and rejoiced. Like Hannah, Mary extolled God for her great blessing and for exalting the poor and bringing down the rich. It is a politically radical prayer. In singing the *Magnificat*, Mary represented Israel's longing for freedom from Rome's oppression. Mary also sings for us who long for the establishment of God's kingdom, the reign of peace and justice. The church prays the *Magnificat* every day in the evening prayer of the Liturgy of the Hours.

Materials

- ☐ Bibles
- ☐ Pens or pencils
- ☐ *The Magnificat* set to music, and a cassette or CD player (optional)
- ☐ Copies of Activity Sheet 5

Activity

1. Ask the children to think of a time when something so wonderful happened that they felt like bursting with joy. Share one of your experiences as an example. Invite the children to share their memories.

2. Explain the context of Mary's *Magnificat* and the significance of its title.
   - Mary was very happy and thankful that God kept his promise and sent a Savior. When she visited Elizabeth, she broke forth in a song-prayer, praising God for choosing her to be his mother. A song-prayer is a canticle.
   - In Mary's canticle, she predicted that from then on everyone would call her blessed. But she knew it was all God's doing. She again called herself God's servant.
   - In Latin, this canticle begins with the word *magnificat,* which means "praise" or "glorify." That is why Mary's canticle is called the *Magnificat*.

3. Tell the children to listen to the *Magnificat* to find three things that Mary praised God for. Read the *Magnificat* from Luke 1:46–55.

4. Distribute Activity Sheet 5. Ask the children for reasons for Mary's praise, letting them refer to the *Magnificat* in their own Bibles. Tell the children to record the reasons on the sheet as they are mentioned. (God chose her, although she was lowly. Everyone will call her blessed. God did great things for her. God has mercy. He scattered the proud, brought down the powerful, and lifted up the lowly. He filled the hungry and sent the rich away empty. He helped Israel by keeping his promise.)

5. Direct the children to write their own *Magnificat* on the sheet. If possible, as they work, play a version of this canticle set to music. When the children are finished, ask for volunteers to share their canticles with the class.

Prayer

My soul glorifies the Lord,
and my spirit rejoices in God my Savior.

Canticles of Praise, Mary's and Mine

In the top section, write reasons Mary praises God in her *Magnificat*.
Then write your own canticle of praise.

My soul magnifies the Lord, and my spirit rejoices in God my Savior, for...

6 HAIL MARY PRAYER: MOTHER OF THE CHURCH

Objective

The children will know the source and meaning of the Hail Mary prayer.

Catechist Notes

The Second Vatican Council's document on the church gave Mary the new title "Mother of the Church." We, her children, honor her and ask her help, assured of an answer. The Hail Mary prayer, the most familiar prayer to Mary, probably originated in the eleventh century. It combines the angel Gabriel's greeting to Mary (with Mary's name inserted) and Elizabeth's greeting. The name "Jesus" was probably inserted in 1262. The ending petition added by the church first appeared in print in 1495. The Hail Mary as we know it today became official in 1568. No doubt your children already know this prayer by heart. This lesson will help them better understand it. Encourage the children who don't know the prayer to use Activity Sheet 6 to memorize it.

Materials

- ☐ Ten large flashcards with phrases of the Hail Mary: *Hail Mary/ full of grace/ the Lord is with you/ blessed are you among women/ and blessed is the fruit of your womb/ Jesus/ Holy Mary/Mother of God/ pray for us sinners/ now and at the hour of our death*
- ☐ Recorded version of the Hail Mary or Ave Maria, such as "Hail Mary: Gentle Woman" by Carey Landry
- ☐ Cassette or CD player
- ☐ Pens or pencils
- ☐ Crayons or felt-tipped pens
- ☐ Copies of Activity Sheet 6

Activity

1. Tell the children that the Hail Mary is the chief prayer to Mary. Then check their familiarity with it. Ask :
   - How many know the Hail Mary by heart?
   - When did you learn it? Who taught it to you?
   - When do you pray it?
2. Give flashcards with phrases of the Hail Mary to ten children. Call them to the front of the room and tell them to arrange themselves in order so that the prayer can be read. Then offer the prayer with all the children.
3. Separate the first three cards and ask where these words came from (the angel Gabriel). Separate the next two cards and ask where these words came from (Elizabeth). Tell the children that the church added the rest of the prayer because we want Mary, our mother, to pray for us.
4. Distribute Activity Sheet 6. Direct the children to match each underlined word in the Hail Mary with its meaning in the box. Correct their answers. **Answers:** *G, B, D, E, H, K, F, J, A, I, C.*
5. Encourage the children to pray the Hail Mary every day. Say, for example: "Mary is the mother of the whole church and your mother too. Try to pray the Hail Mary each night before you go to bed. That way, you will think of our mother Mary, honor her, and ask her help every day."
6. Play a recorded version of the Hail Mary.

Prayer

Mary, you are the greatest woman that ever lived. Pray for me, your child, that I may be holy like you.

The Hail Mary Prayer

Below each underlined word or phrase, write the letter of its meaning found in the box. Then draw pretty things around the prayer, such as flowers and butterflies.

Hail Mary,

full of grace, the Lord is with you.

Blessed are you among women,

and blessed is the fruit of your womb,

Jesus.

Holy Mary, Mother of God,

pray for us sinners now

and at the hour of our death.

Amen.

A	ask God for something
B	divine (God's) life
C	end of life when we most need prayer
D	almighty God
E	favored by God
F	pure and loving like God
G	hello
H	your baby
I	those who disobey God
J	woman who gave birth to the Savior
K	the Savior

7 BIRTH OF JESUS, MOTHER OF GOD

Objective

The children will review the story of how Mary became the Mother of God in Bethlehem.

Catechist Notes

The birth of Jesus was a wondrous and unique event. Mary, a virgin, had a baby who was both divine and human. Her Son would grow up to save the world from sin. The remarkable events surrounding the nativity of Jesus in the gospels are a mix of hardship and glory. Even though she was nine months pregnant, Mary traveled to Bethlehem in obedience to the government edict. There she gave birth in the only shelter available, a place where animals are kept, probably a cave. Yet that night angels filled the skies and shepherds came to worship. Later, wise men from the East brought gifts for Mary's Son.

Materials

- ☐ Bible
- ☐ A wrapped gift
- ☐ Long flashcard with "Jesus is the reason for the season" displayed so the blank side shows
- ☐ A nativity set or flashcards with these words: *Mary, Joseph, child Jesus, manger, shepherds, angels, wise men*
- ☐ Pens or pencils
- ☐ Copies of Activity Sheet 7

Activity

1. Show the gift and discuss the meaning of Christmas.
   - On Christmas Day, we give and receive gifts. What gifts have you gotten on Christmas?
   - What do we celebrate on Christmas? (the birth of Jesus, the Savior) Jesus is the best gift of all. He is the gift of God the Father to us. On Christmas night about two thousand years ago, Mary gave birth to Jesus. [Turn over the flashcard with "Jesus is the reason for the season."]
   - Each year we remember the story. We read it in the gospels, and we sing hymns about it.
2. Sing "Silent Night" with the children. (You might have to teach it.)
3. Give children the nativity set figures (or the flashcards). Tell them that you will read the story of the Nativity. When they hear the word for the figure (or flashcard) they have, they are to hold it up. Then read Luke 2:1–20 and Matthew 2:1–12.
4. Tell the children that Saint Francis of Assisi was the first one to recreate the nativity scene. He used live animals. Today, nativity scenes are found in churches and homes.
5. Direct the children to set the nativity figures in place in front of the room (or display the flashcards). Comment:
   - The gospel says that Mary pondered in her heart everything that happened when Jesus was born. That means she thought hard about it. Each Christmas, we too ponder God's love in sending his Son.
6. Distribute Activity Sheet 7 and have the children work the crossword puzzle. Check their answers. **Answers:** *Across: 2) king; 5) manger; 9) star; 10) Bethlehem; 11) inn; 12) Herod; 14) glory; 15) Joseph. Down: 1) wisemen; 3) Mary; 4) angels; 6) shepherds; 7) David; 8) sheep; 13) ox.*

Prayer

Dear Mary, Mother of God, thank you for bringing our Savior into the world.

The First Christmas

Use the clues to fill in the Christmas crossword puzzle.

ACROSS

2 Jesus was the new _____ of the Jews.

5 Crib of Baby Jesus

9 It led the wise men to Jesus.

10 Town where Jesus was born

11 It had no room for Mary and Joseph

12 King who wanted to see Jesus

14 Angels sang "_____ to God."

15 Mary's husband

DOWN

1 Came from the East to see the new king

3 The mother of God

4 They appeared in the sky.

6 First people to visit Jesus

7 Bethlehem was the city of _____, Joseph's ancestor.

8 What shepherds were likely watching.

13 Animal that may have been in the stable.

8 PRESENTATION OF JESUS: MOTHER OF SORROWS

Objective

The children will learn that Mary's life was marked with hardships.

Catechist Notes

Luke's gospel combines two customs that Jewish law required. The first was the presentation of Jesus as the firstborn son, who had to be redeemed by paying forty shekels. This was the time of circumcision and naming. The second custom was Mary's purification, which entailed a sacrifice forty days after the birth of a son. This is the first time Jesus entered the temple. Simeon and Anna were holy Israelites who trusted in God's promise of a savior. The gist of the gospel story is that Mary learns that her Son will be a light for the Gentiles, but that both Jesus and Mary will suffer.

Materials

- ☐ Paper: a yellow sheet with a happy face, a red sheet with a frowning face and tears
- ☐ Pens or pencils
- ☐ Copies of Activity Sheet 8

Activity

1. Discuss happy and sad events.
    - Each day, things happen that make us happy. Each day, bad or sad things happen too. Maybe this morning you had your favorite breakfast. [Show the happy face.] But then you missed the school bus. [Show the sad face.]
    - What happy things have happened to you? As you answer, hold the happy face and then pass it to the next child who answers.
    - What sad things happened to you? As you answer, hold the red sheet and then pass it on.

2. Tell the story of the presentation.
    - One special day was a mixture of happiness and sadness for Mary.
    - Shortly after Jesus was born, Mary and Joseph took him to the temple. They presented him to God and sacrificed two birds, according to Jewish law.
    - Simeon was a good man who looked forward to the Messiah. The Holy Spirit revealed to him that he wouldn't die until he saw the Messiah. When Jesus was in the temple, the Holy Spirit inspired Simeon to go there. Simeon held baby Jesus. He prayed that God would let him die in peace now because he had seen salvation. Simeon called Jesus a light for the Gentiles (non-Jews) and the glory of the Jewish people.
    - Simeon told Mary that people would reject Jesus, and a sword would pierce her too, meaning that she would have sorrow.
    - Anna, an old prophet who lived in the temple, saw Jesus. She praised God and told everyone about the Messiah who had come.

3. Ask what made Mary happy that day. (It was confirmed that her Son was the Messiah. He came for everyone.) Ask what made Mary sad. (She and her Son would suffer.) Comment:
    - You might expect that because Mary was holy and God chose her to be his mother, her life was easy. Instead, she suffered like us.

4. Distribute Activity Sheet 8. Tell the children that Simeon's words came true. Direct them to draw a smile in the circle for something happy and a frown for something sad. Check their work. **Answers:** *Happy events are 1, 2, 5, 7, 9, 12, 15.*

Prayer

Mary, Mother of sorrows, pray that I put my sorrows to good use by offering them to God for an intention.

Mother of Sorrows

Read each event in Mary's life listed here. If it is happy, draw a smiling face. If it is sad, draw a frowning face.

1. Mary learns that her Son is the Savior of the world.

2. Shepherds and wise men from the East honor baby Jesus.

3. Simeon foretells that people will reject Jesus.

4. The Holy Family must flee to Egypt because King Herod wants Jesus killed.

5. Mary cooks, makes clothes for, and teaches the child Jesus at home in Nazareth.

6. Jesus is lost for three days in Jerusalem.

7. Jesus learns to be a carpenter like Joseph.

8. After Jesus speaks in Nazareth, his neighbors try to throw him off a cliff.

9. Jesus works miracles to help people, especially the sick.

10. People say that Jesus is crazy and possessed by the devil.

11. Religious leaders criticize and scold Jesus.

12. Jesus feeds thousands of people by multiplying bread and fish.

13. Jesus is condemned to death, and Mary meets him as he carries his cross.

14. Jesus dies on the cross and is laid in a tomb.

15. Jesus rises from the dead.

9 FLIGHT INTO EGYPT: REFUGEE

Objective

The children will understand the difficulties the flight into Egypt posed for Mary.

Catechist Notes

The flight into Egypt is one of the seven traditional sorrows of Mary. It foreshadows the rejection that Jesus will face as he carries out his mission. It also parallels how the Israelites came out of Egypt after having been spared the death of their firstborn. Apocryphal writings tell of miracles occurring when the Holy Family fled. Palm trees bent so the family could reach their fruit, animals paid homage to Jesus, and Egyptian idols crashed down before him. In Egypt, several churches and shrines supposedly stand on sites where the Holy Family stayed. The account of the flight into Egypt is only found in chapter 2 of Matthew's gospel. Herod was a vicious ruler who had his uncle, wife, and three sons murdered to protect his throne. His slaughtering of Bethlehem infants is plausible. Scholars surmise that there would have been about twenty children killed. If possible, show the children a picture of a statue that is in the lower level of the Basilica of the Immaculate Conception in Washington, which shows the Holy Family and their donkey all asleep.

Materials

- ☐ A WHEEL WITH SPOKES AND A HUB THAT SAYS "MOVING" DRAWN ON THE BOARD OR ON POSTER PAPER
- ☐ CHALK OR FELT-TIPPED PEN
- ☐ ARTWORK DEPICTING THE FLIGHT INTO EGYPT.
- ☐ COPIES OF ACTIVITY SHEET 9

Activity

1. Tell the children to raise their hands if their family has ever moved to another place. Ask the children to name some difficulties and problems to solve when moving, and write their answers on the spokes of a wheel drawn on the board. (Possible answers: packing, traveling, finding a house, father or mother getting a new job, learning where to shop, making new friends)

2. Define refugees.
   - Some people must move to another country to escape danger or to be free. They are called refugees. What refugees do you know of? (Answers will vary.)
   - Mary, Joseph, and baby Jesus were once refugees.

3. Show artwork of the flight into Egypt and introduce the event.
   - One of Mary's sorrows was fleeing to Egypt to save baby Jesus' life. King Herod was afraid that a new king would replace him. When the wise men came looking for the newborn king, Herod decided to kill Jesus.

4. Distribute copies of Activity Sheet 9. Call on children to read aloud the imaginary letter from Mary to her parents in Nazareth.

5. Inform the children that:
   - In Egypt an angel spoke to Joseph in a dream again. He told Joseph to return because Herod was dead. The Holy Family went to Nazareth.
   - We celebrate the Feast of the Holy Innocents (the babies martyred) on December 28.

Prayer

Jesus, Mary, and Joseph, come to the aid of today's refugees. See that they are safe and receive what they need to live well.

The Holy Family Flees

Imagine that Mary asked a scribe, a secretary, to write to her parents while she was in Egypt. The letter below might be what she would have written. Read it.

Dear Mother and Father,

You will be surprised that I'm writing from Egypt. While we were still in Bethlehem, Joseph woke me up during the night and said we had to flee. In a dream an angel had told him that Herod was going to hunt for Jesus to kill him. I hurriedly gathered our clothes and some bread and fruit. My heart was pounding. Soon we set out, with me and Jesus riding our donkey and only the stars to guide Joseph. We would travel more than a hundred miles to save Jesus.

The journey was tiresome and unpleasant for a little baby. The roads were rough, and the sun was hot. We couldn't risk stopping for long. I kept thinking I heard Herod's soldiers coming after us.

When we reached Egypt, we stayed at an inn. Then Joseph found a little house and we bought it with the money we had left. To support us, Joseph got a job working on a fortress. His tools were back in Nazareth, so he had to buy new ones. I couldn't have married a better man.

I made friends with some women at the well. They told me the best places to shop at the market. They also gave me some tips for taking care of an infant. Still, I miss you both and my friends in Nazareth.

Shortly after we arrived here, we heard horrible news. Herod wanted to make sure that Jesus was dead. He had his soldiers kill all infants two years old and younger in and around Bethlehem. My heart breaks for their mothers and fathers.

I don't know when it will be safe to return. I'm not looking forward to another long trip. But every day I thank God that my son is still alive. Jesus is such a good and happy baby. I also ask God to keep all of us safe.

I think of you every day and hope you are well. God willing, we will see one another again soon and you can meet your grandson.

Your loving daughter,

Mary

10 FINDING OF JESUS IN THE TEMPLE: MOTHER OF JESUS

Objective

The children will see that Mary loved her Son but was puzzled by him.

Catechist Notes

Finding Jesus in the temple is the only gospel story about him from the time between when the Holy Family returned to Nazareth and the time he left home to begin his ministry. Like a typical youth, Jesus caused his parents distress. But he was extraordinary in astounding the teachers with his knowledge. He revealed his divine nature by calling the temple his Father's house. We can imagine Mary's guilt for not missing Jesus in the caravan and her anguish during the hunt for him. This event is both one of her seven traditional sorrows and the fifth joyful mystery of the Rosary.

Materials

- ☐ PENS, PENCILS, CRAYONS, OR FELT-TIPPED PENS
- ☐ COPIES OF ACTIVITY SHEET 10

Activity

1. Ask the children if they ever got lost or strayed away from their mother. Invite a few to tell about it and how their mothers felt. Then comment:
   - Jesus was twelve and the family went to the holy city Jerusalem for the Passover feast. When the families left Jerusalem, Jesus stayed behind in the temple to talk with the teachers. Mary lost her Son for three long days and nights.

2. Lead the children in guided prayer.
   - Mary, like any mother, cared for her child, helped him learn to walk and talk, washed his clothes, and prepared his food. Today we will think about the time when Jesus was lost. This is a form of praying.
   - Close your eyes. Picture Mary walking home from Jerusalem with a group of people. That evening, Joseph comes to her. She asks, "Where is Jesus?" Joseph replies, "He is probably with relatives and friends." Both search in vain for Jesus among the travelers. Finally, Joseph says, "We must go back to Jerusalem." They leave the caravan and walk to the city.
   - The next morning, Mary and Joseph are in Jerusalem. See them knocking on doors and stopping people in the street to ask if they've seen Jesus. They do this for two days. See how worried they look.
   - Mary and Joseph go into the magnificent temple. There is Jesus, sitting and talking with teachers. Mary scolds, "Child, why have you treated us like this? Your father and I have been worried sick." Jesus says, "Why were you looking for me? Didn't you know I must be in my Father's house?" Mary and Joseph look at each other and shrug. They don't know what Jesus means.
   - Joseph says to Jesus, "Let's go home now." He puts his arm around Jesus' shoulders, and the three leave the temple. From then on Jesus obeys Mary and Joseph.
   - Open your eyes. What did Jesus mean by being in his Father's house? (The temple was God's house, and Jesus was God's Son.)

3. Distribute Activity Sheet 10. Direct the children to create a missing child poster for Jesus.

Prayer

Mary, you didn't understand why Jesus frightened you. When things happen that I don't understand, pray that I still trust in God's love for me.

A Lost Child

Design a missing person poster for the boy Jesus. Include his name, a picture, what he looks like, what he was wearing, where he was from, who his parents are, and where he was last seen.

11 WEDDING OF CANA: INTERCESSOR

Objective

The children will ask Mary to pray for them when they are in need.

Catechist Notes

The story of the wedding feast in Cana (John 2:1–11) is an account of Mary jumpstarting Jesus' public ministry. In deference to his mother, Jesus worked his first miracle. This event highlights Mary's quick response to others' needs and her ability to influence God. It illustrates her willingness to go to her Son and intercede for others. Jesus addressing Mary as "woman" may be a sign that she is a new Eve, who brings forth new life. He called her "woman" again from the cross. The wine Jesus produced was excellent and abundant—about one hundred and fifty gallons. It signifies the magnificence of God's kingdom.

Materials

- ☐ HIGHLIGHTER
- ☐ PROPS FOR PLAY (OPTIONAL): TUREEN OR PITCHER, LADLE, MUG
- ☐ CLAY OR ALUMINUM FOIL
- ☐ COPIES OF ACTIVITY SHEET 11, ONE FOR EACH CAST MEMBER, WITH PARTS HIGHLIGHTED

Activity

1. Explain Mary as intercessor.
   - Ask the children when they might seek something on behalf of someone else. Provide an example, such as asking a group of friends to include a new student in a game. Explain that this is called "interceding." To intercede means to ask for something on someone else's behalf.
   - Explain that we call Mary an "intercessor." When we turn to Mary, we ask for her prayers on our behalf and on behalf of all of those who are suffering or in need.
2. Introduce the play about the wedding at Cana.
   - One gospel event shows what a powerful intercessor Mary is. It also shows that when Mary is aware of a problem, she acts to solve it.
3. Choose children for the roles in the play and give them copies of Activity Sheet 11. Let them look over their parts and the stage directions. Then have them act out the play or simply read their parts while you read the stage directions.
4. Discuss the play.
   - How would the newlyweds and their parents feel if their guests weren't able to drink more wine? (sad, humiliated)
   - How did Mary act as an intercessor? (She went to her Son for help.)
   - It wasn't time yet for Jesus to begin his ministry in public. Why, then, did he work this miracle? (He couldn't refuse his mother.)
   - Mary said something that can be called her commandment. What was it? ("Do whatever he tells you," meaning, obey Jesus.)
5. Give the children clay or aluminum foil and have them shape a water jar. Encourage them to keep their jar where they can see it and be reminded to go to Mary when in need.

Prayer

Mary, you love me and are eager to help when I have a problem. I ask you to please pray that...

Water into Wine

A PLAY*

CAST: Narrator, Jesus, Mary, Bride, Groom, Headwaiter; Disciples 1 and 2, Servants 1 and 2; Guests

(Jesus, Disciples, and Guests stand talking. Mary speaks to the Bride, and the Headwaiter to the Groom. Servants 1 and 2 stand together.)

NARRATOR: Mary, Jesus, and his disciples were guests at a wedding in Cana in Galilee. The servants realized there was a problem.

SERVANT 1: The wine ran out. What can we do?

SERVANT 2: I don't know. How embarrassing for the family!

(Mary goes to Jesus. The Bride and Groom speak together.)

MARY *(to Jesus)*: They have no wine.

JESUS: Woman, what concern is that to you and to me? My hour has not yet come.

MARY *(walks over to Servants)*: Do whatever he tells you.

JESUS *(to Servants)*: Fill those jars with water.

NARRATOR *(while Servants fill the jars)*: Six stone water jars used for ritual washings were standing there. Each held about twenty-five gallons. The servants filled them to the brim.

JESUS *(to Servants)*: Now draw out some water and take it to the headwaiter.

(Servant 1 ladles water into mug and takes it to the Headwaiter.)

SERVANT 1: Sir, would you taste this wine, please?

(Headwaiter takes a sip and gestures to Groom to come.)

HEADWAITER *(to Groom)*: This is delicious. Everyone serves good wine first and cheaper wine when the guests have drunk a lot. But you have saved the good wine until now.

DISCIPLE 1 *(to Disciple 2)*: Did you see that?

DISCIPLE 2: I think we can believe this man Jesus.

NARRATOR: Jesus worked his first miracle at the request of his mother, Mary. When we have a special favor to pray for, let us ask Mary to add her prayer to ours.

* Adapted from *Gospel Theater for the Whole Community: 92 Plays for Education and Worship* by Mary Kathleen Glavich, SND (Twenty-Third Publications)

12 MARY VISITS JESUS: LISTENING VIRGIN

Objective

The children will understand that Mary lives as God teaches.

Catechist Notes

The synoptic gospels all mention a time when Jesus taught that anyone who obeys God's word belongs to his family. Because that statement was prompted by the news that the mother and brothers of Jesus wanted to see him, it could be interpreted as a snub of his natural family. Yet who more than his mother, Mary, lived according to God's word?

Materials

- ☐ Bible
- ☐ A manual for a piece of equipment
- ☐ Pens or pencils
- ☐ Copies of Activity Sheet 12

Activity

1. Show a manual for a piece of equipment. Compare it to God's will for us.
   - Who drew up the manual? (the manufacturer)
   - What is the purpose of a manual? (to give directions for assembling and using something)
   - What might happen if the manual's instructions aren't followed? (Equipment might not be put together correctly or break.)
   - God is our maker and knows best how we should live well. Mary understood this and always listened to God.
   - One day, Jesus taught about the importance of doing God's will.

2. Read Mark 3:31–35, the account of Mary coming to Jesus while he was teaching. Then discuss:
   - Why does it seem like Jesus was unkind to his mother and relatives? (Instead of welcoming them, he says that his disciples are his family.)
   - Jesus teaches that those who do God's will are like his family. This is not a putdown of Mary, because it includes Mary. What are some times when Mary did what God wanted? (when she agreed to be God's mother, when she showed love for Elizabeth by helping her, when she and Joseph obeyed the government and went to Bethlehem, when they obeyed the religious law and took Jesus to the temple for the presentation)
   - Your family members, the people closest to you, are important to you. In the time of Jesus, families were very important. For Jesus to say that obeying God makes us part of his family is wonderful.

3. Explain why the story refers to the brothers and sisters of Jesus.
   - The Catholic Church teaches that Mary was always a virgin and never had other children. Why then does this Scripture passage refer to the sisters and brothers of Jesus? Perhaps because Aramaic, the language Jesus spoke, had no word for cousin, the writer substituted "brothers and sisters." Some scholars think that Joseph might have been a widower with children. Then Jesus would have had stepbrothers and stepsisters.

4. Distribute Activity Sheet 12. Tell the children that the headings on the chart are ways that God makes his will known. Direct them to write an example of what God might be saying to them through each way. The children might work in pairs.

5. Invite the children to share their answers with the rest of the class.

Prayer

Jesus, I want to belong to your family.
Grant me the grace to listen to you and then to act on your words as Mary did.

Doing What God Wants

Under each heading, write something that God might tell you to do through that channel.

The Bible

Our parents or those who act as parents for us

The Church

The law

The homily at Mass

Our teachers

Speak, Lord, for your servant is listening.

1 SAMUEL 3:9

13 MARY ON CALVARY: OUR BLESSED MOTHER

Objective

The children will love Mary as their heavenly mother and be introduced to the *Memorare*.

Catechist Notes

Mary is our mother on the spiritual plane. Through her cooperation with God, which involved much suffering, she brought forth the Savior, enabling us to receive divine life and be born anew. As God's adopted children, we are brothers and sisters of Mary's Son, Jesus. She who gave birth to Jesus physically is now mother to his mystical body. In a poem, Gerard Manley Hopkins, SJ, wrote that Mary "mothers each new grace/that now does reach our race." If your children are not likely to add spontaneous intentions during the prayer service, instead they might write requests on slips of paper ahead of time and deposit them in a basket before Mary's image.

Materials

- ☐ Bible
- ☐ An image of Mary
- ☐ A candle and matches or an electric candle
- ☐ Recording of a hymn to Mary
- ☐ Cassette or CD player
- ☐ Copies of Activity Sheet 13

Activity

1. Invite the children to take turns miming something their mother does for them, and have the rest of the class guess what it is. (Possible actions are cooking, sewing, driving, loving, cheering for them, drying their tears, praying for them.)

2. State that when Jesus was dying, he gave his mother, Mary, to us as our mother. Then read John 19:25–27. Explain:
   - The disciple Jesus loved is often assumed to be Saint John. He stands for all of us. Therefore, Jesus made his mother our mother. The church also teaches us that Mary is our mother.

3. Compare Mary to earthly mothers.
   - Mary, our heavenly mother, acts toward us the way earthly mothers act toward their children:

   She risked her life so that we could have eternal, spiritual life.
   She is a model for us, showing us how to live a good life.
   She suffered for us, especially when her Son died to save us.
   She is always ready to help us.
   She prays to God for us.
   Her dream for us is that we may be with her safely in heaven.
   She loves us deeply.

4. Introduce the *Memorare*.
   - A very old prayer to Mary is the *Memorare*. Its name is from the prayer's first word, *remember*, which in Latin is *memorare*. In the *Memorare*, we ask Mary our mother to grant our requests.

5. Distribute copies of Activity Sheet 13. Appoint children to be a leader and a reader. Tell them that there will be time at the end of the prayer service for them to speak their own intentions to Mary. Light a candle before an image of Mary. Then conduct the prayer service.

Prayer

Mary, my mother, thank you for your loving care. Help me to be a faithful child of God and to follow your model of holiness.

Our Blessed Mother

A PRAYER SERVICE

(Light a candle by an image of the Blessed Mother.)

SONG:
A hymn to Mary

SCRIPTURE READING
John 19:25–27

PRAYER *(The Memorare)*
Remember, O most gracious Virgin Mary,
that never was it known that anyone
who fled to your protection,
implored your help, or sought your
intercession was left unaided.
Inspired by this confidence, I fly unto
you, O Virgin of virgins, my Mother.
To you I come, before you I stand,
sinful and sorrowful.
O Mother of the Word incarnate,
despise not my petitions,
but in your mercy hear
and answer me. Amen.

PETITIONS

Side 1: Mary, you always obeyed God.
Help me do what God knows is best.
Side 2: Mary, you loved your Son, Jesus.
Pray for me so that my love for him
grows each day.
Side 1: Mary, you reached out to others
who were in need.
Help me to respond with love
when my family members
and others need help.
Side 2: Mary, you were a good citizen
of your country.
Ask God to bless my country.
Side 1: Mary, you suffered much in your life
as Mother of God.
Pray that I have patience
when I undergo trials and pain.
Side 2: Mary, hear us as we pray...
(add intentions)

PRAYER
Hail Mary, full of grace, the Lord is with you.
Blessed are you among women
and blessed is the fruit of your womb, Jesus.
Holy Mary, Mother of God, pray for us sinners
now and at the hour of our death. Amen.

"Mary is more mother than queen."
ST. THÉRÈSE OF LISIEUX

14 PENTECOST: OUR LADY, STAR OF EVANGELIZATION

Objective

The children will know that the Holy Spirit acted in Mary as she guided the church.

Catechist Notes

As the church embarked on a new evangelization effort, Mary received her latest title, Our Lady, Star of Evangelization, reflecting her role as proto-evangelizer. An evangelizer spreads the good news about Jesus. Mary first brought the news of the Savior to Elizabeth. Then at Pentecost, the same Holy Spirit who overshadowed Mary at the Annunciation filled her. Presumably she spent the rest of her life telling the early church members about her Son and supporting them as they spread the word.

Materials

- ☐ A Bible
- ☐ Candle and matches (or a picture of fire)
- ☐ Crayons or felt-tipped pens
- ☐ Copies of Activity Sheet 14

Activity

1. Light the candle. Ask the children for words related to fire (warmth, heat, beauty, guidance, purification, melting, power, destruction). Comment:
   - Fire is a symbol for the Holy Spirit. Today you will learn why.
2. Present Mary as an evangelizer.
   - On the day Jesus returned to heaven, he told his disciples to evangelize. That means to spread the good news about him to the whole world.
   - The risen Jesus instructed his disciples to wait in Jerusalem for the Holy Spirit. They did as Jesus said and prayed. Mary was with them.
   - Mary was the first evangelizer. When the Holy Spirit overshadowed her, she became pregnant with Jesus. Then she carried Jesus within her to her cousin Elizabeth. On Pentecost, the Holy Spirit came to her again.
3. Read the coming of the Holy Spirit on Pentecost from Acts 2:1–6. Then discuss:
   - The power of God came over Mary and the other disciples. They had the courage and wisdom to tell other people about Jesus and make them disciples too.
   - The day this happened was Pentecost. It is called the birthday of the church. So Mary was present when the church made its public appearance. The other disciples looked to her as their mother.
   - The men disciples like Saint Peter went out and preached to crowds about Jesus.
   - Whom do you think Mary talked to about Jesus? (the disciples, her friends, people she met at the well or in the market)
4. Discuss Mary as the Star of Evangelization.
   - A star has two meanings. What are they? (a ball of burning gas, a person famous for his or her talent)
   - Why do you think that Mary has the new title Star of Evangelization? (She was one of the best evangelizers; she guided others like stars do; she gives light; she is on fire with the Holy Spirit.)
5. Distribute Activity Sheet 14. Remark that artists represent the Holy Spirit as a dove because the gospels say that at Jesus' baptism the Spirit came down like a dove. Direct the children to draw a picture of Mary. Encourage them to pray to her as they work.

Prayer

Mary, Star of Evangelization, ask the Holy Spirit to give me power and courage to spread the Good News too.

The Holy Spirit's Coming to the Church

Draw a picture of Mary beneath the flames.
Color the flames. As you work, pray:
"Mary, Star of Evangelization,
pray for me."

15 ASSUMPTION: SAINT MARY

Objective

The children will understand that Mary went to heaven body and soul.

Catechist Notes

Pentecost is the last time the Bible mentions Mary by name. It's assumed that she either lived in Jerusalem, or went with Saint John to Ephesus. The doctrine of the Assumption is that when Mary's life was ended, she was taken to heaven body and soul. This doctrine was declared in 1950, although the church had believed it for centuries. The eastern church calls the passing of Mary the *dormition* or sleeping away.

Materials

- ☐ Seeds
- ☐ Scissors and tape or glue
- ☐ Green chenille sticks
- ☐ Green and yellow construction paper
- ☐ Copies of Activity Sheet 16 on heavy white paper

Activity

1. Show seeds and compare their death to ours.
   - Have you ever planted seeds? What did they become?
   - A seed must die before it becomes a plant with flowers, fruit, or vegetables.
   - We too have to die in order to have new, eternal life.
   - At the end of the world, our bodies will be reunited with our souls. They will be glorified like the risen body of Jesus was.

2. Introduce the Assumption.
   - At the end of her life, Mary was taken immediately to heaven, body and soul. We say she was "assumed" into heaven.
   - The Assumption of Mary is a doctrine of the faith. We celebrate it on August 15, which is a holy day of obligation.
   - Imagine how happy Mary was to see her Son, Jesus, again and know they would never be separated.
   - We too hope to see Jesus in heaven someday just as Mary has done.

3. Tell a legend about Mary's death.
   - There is a lovely legend about Mary's death. In the story, an angel tells Mary that she will be brought to heaven in three days. Mary asks for the apostles to be with her at her death. Miraculously, they all arrive in time. When they bury Mary, Jesus appears, and angels take her to heaven. One version says that the apostle Thomas was late. When the apostles take him to Mary's tomb and open it, instead of her body, they find roses and lilies.

4. Distribute Activity Sheet 15. Guide the children in making lilies. You might display the lilies on a bulletin board to represent Mary's empty tomb.

Prayer

Jesus, your mother was the first to be with you body and soul. May I live in such a way that I will join you some day.

Mary's Assumption

The lily is a symbol for Mary. Its pure white color reminds us that she is without sin. The gold stamens represent her royalty. Make a lily.

DIRECTIONS

① Cut out the rectangle and fold it in half.

② Fold the folded left side over on a diagonal one third of the way and then fold the right side over this.

③ At the bottom of the valley at the top, cut a straight line and remove the top piece.

④ Cut a peak at the top and open the paper.

⑤ Curl each petal by pulling it between a scissor blade and your thumb.

⑥ Tape the two end petals together.

⑦ Out of yellow paper cut three stamens like matchsticks and insert them and the stem, a green chenille stick, into the lily.

⑧ Cut leaves from green paper, and tape or glue them to the stem.

16 CORONATION: QUEEN OF THE UNIVERSE

Objective

The children will honor Mary as queen.

Catechist Notes

When Mary was assumed into heaven, she was crowned queen of heaven and earth. Some paintings depict the Trinity crowning her. She's been called queen at least since the fourth century. In his encyclical *Ad Caeli Reginam* (To the Queen of Heaven), Pope Pius XII offers reasons for Mary's coronation: She is mother of the Creator, she is associated with her Son's redemption, she is perfect, and she has intercessory powers. The Second Vatican Council gave her a new title: Queen of the Universe. The feast of the Queenship of Mary is August 22. For the crowning of Mary in this lesson, you might teach the children a hymn to Mary ahead of time.

Materials

- ☐ Words on the board or poster paper: *Totus Tuus* and *consecration*
- ☐ A statue of Mary
- ☐ A crown for the statue
- ☐ Two recorded hymns to Mary, such as "Hail, Holy Queen"
- ☐ Cassette or CD player
- ☐ Copies of Activity Sheet 16

Activity

1. Show the crown and discuss queenship.
   - Who wears a crown? (kings and queens)
   - What is a queen? (a woman who rules a country, the wife or mother of a king)
   - The Israelites considered the king's mother to be the most powerful queen.
   - Sometimes we call a woman who is the best at something a "queen," like "the 'queen' of country music."
2. Present Mary as queen.
   - Mary is the mother of Jesus, the King, and is a powerful intercessor, or speaker, for us.
   - After Mary was assumed body and soul into heaven, she was crowned queen of heaven and earth. She is queen of the whole universe.
   - Who is Mary a queen of? (us, angels, all the saints, the apostles)
3. Distribute copies of Activity Sheet 16. Explain the crowning of an image of the Blessed Virgin Mary.
   - The church has a special ritual to honor Mary as queen. We pray and sing to her and crown a statue of her.
   - By this ritual we show Mary that we honor her.
4. Prepare for the crowning. Choose a child to crown the statue. Assign a reader. Designate the sides.
5. Explain a consecration to Mary.
   - Popes and bishops have a motto, words they live by. Pope Saint John Paul II's motto was *Totus Tuus,* which is Latin for "All yours." He meant he was giving himself and all his work to Mary.
   - Giving ourselves to God or Mary is called "consecration." When we give ourselves to Mary, we are really giving ourselves to Jesus.
   - In the crowning ceremony, we will consecrate ourselves to Mary.
6. Carry out the crowning of Mary.

Prayer

Mary, you are queen of the universe and my queen. Please ask your Son to bring peace to the world and to my family.

Crowning Mary, Our Queen

SONG: "Hail, Holy Queen"
or another Marian hymn

ALL: O God, you have given us Mary, the mother of your Son, as our mother and queen. Grant that we who will crown her image today may someday be with you and Mary in your kingdom of heaven. Amen.

READING: Luke 1:26–38

ALL:
Blessed are you, O God,
for your Son who died on the cross
is with you now in glory.
He is the King of Kings and Lord of Lords.
And his mother, Mary,
  who called herself your servant,
now reigns in glory with her Son,
  praying for all of us.
By crowning this image of Mary,
  we honor her as our queen.
Give us the grace to imitate her
  and serve you.
We ask this through Christ, our Lord. Amen.

Crowning of Mary

Litany to Mary

SIDE 1: Holy Mary, pray for us.
SIDE 2: Holy Mother of God, pray for us.
SIDE 1: Queen of love, pray for us.
SIDE 2: Queen of mercy, pray for us.
SIDE 1: Queen of peace, pray for us.
SIDE 2: Queen of angels, pray for us.
SIDE 1: Queen of apostles, pray for us.
SIDE 2: Queen of all saints, pray for us.
SIDE 1: Queen conceived without original sin, pray for us.
SIDE 2: Queen assumed into heaven, pray for us.
SIDE 1: Queen of heaven and earth, pray for us.
SIDE 2: Queen of the universe, pray for us.
SIDE 1: Pray for us, O glorious Mother of the Lord.
SIDE 2: That we may become worthy of the promises of Christ.

Consecration to Mary

ALL: My queen, my mother, I give myself entirely to you. And to show my devotion to you, I consecrate to you this day my eyes, my ears, my mouth, my heart, my whole being without reserve. Wherefore, good mother, as I am your own, keep me and guard me as your property and possession. Amen.

SONG: A Marian hymn

17 WOMAN OF THE BOOK OF REVELATION: VIRGIN MOST POWERFUL

Objective

The children will be acquainted with the woman in Revelation considered to be Mary.

Catechist Notes

The Book of Revelation was written to assure persecuted Christians that God will be victorious. It is an account of John's visions. In one vision, he sees a pregnant woman in heaven. A dragon waits to devour her newborn son, but God saves him. This woman is interpreted to be Israel or the church, but most popularly she stands for the Blessed Virgin. In this lesson, the children view Mary as a helper in dealing with temptation. As St. Bernard of Clairvaux advised: "If the winds of temptation arise...look at the star, call upon Mary." The children might enjoy drawing the red dragon or the pregnant woman with a crown of twelve stars.

Materials

- ☐ Pictures of symbols that stand for something else, such as a heart (symbol of love); tree (symbol of family ancestry); flag (symbol of a country); Statue of Liberty (symbol of freedom)
- ☐ A Bible
- ☐ Pens or pencils
- ☐ Copies of Activity Sheet 17

Activity

1. Show the symbols and discuss what they mean. Draw upon answers that describe how symbols stand for something else.
   - Point out that the Bible contains many symbols. The Book of Revelation describes visions of a man named John. They are as fantastic as fairy tales. The book is full of symbols.
   - In one of John's visions is a woman who is thought to stand for Mary.
2. Tell the children to picture the story as you read it and to listen for reasons why the woman could represent Mary. Then read Revelation 12:1–6.
3. Ask how the woman is like Mary. Mention these points if the children do not:
   - She is glorious like a queen.
   - She gives birth to a son who will rule the world.
   - The dragon tries to kill her son, just as Herod tried to kill Jesus.
   - She and her child are protected by God.
4. Present Mary as a powerful help against temptation.
   - The vision ends with the dragon making war on the woman's other children. Who might they be? (us)
   - Who does the dragon represent? (the devil) The devil was thrown out of heaven. He does not want us to be there, so he tempts us to disobey God.
   - The woman in the story escaped the dragon. Mary's Son saved us from the power of sin. When we are tempted to turn away from God, Mary can pray for us. Her Son listens to her and gives us the strength to be good and loving.
5. Distribute Activity Sheet 17. Instruct the children to write two ways we might be tempted to turn away from God, and then write a prayer to Mary for her intercession. When they are finished, invite them to share what they have written.

Prayer

Mary, you are the sinless one who brought our Savior into the world. When we are tempted, pray that we have the strength to resist.

Mary, Our Help in Temptation

Write two things that might tempt us to turn away from God.
Then, in the star, write a prayer to Mary asking for her intercession.

TEMPTATION 1

TEMPTATION 2

18 MARY, OUR MODEL, THE FIRST AND BEST DISCIPLE

Objective

The children will aim to live like Mary, who followed Jesus' teachings.

Catechist Notes

In a prayer, Cardinal Merry del Val told Mary that she teaches him all that he has to know: what Jesus is for him and what he ought to be for Jesus. St. Louis de Montfort called Mary "the mold of God." Looking at Mary, we learn what it means to follow Jesus with all our heart. Although Mary was sinless, imitating her is not impossible. We too can heed what God calls us to do—trust in God and his love for us, and love God and others.

Materials

- ☐ Prize, such as a holy card or statue of Mary
- ☐ Pens or pencils
- ☐ Copies of Activity Sheet 18

Activity

1. Ask what a disciple is. (a person who believes in Jesus, learns his teachings, and lives by them) Tell the children that whoever answers first will win a prize. Ask who was Jesus' first disciple. (Mary) Award the prize. Clarify:
   - Mary was the first to hear that Jesus was the Savior. Who told her? (the angel Gabriel) She lived with Jesus about thirty years, so she probably learned much from him.
   - Mary lived what Jesus taught. She is his first disciple.

2. Present Mary as our model.
   - Mothers teach us how to live. Mary, our heavenly mother, teaches us how to be a disciple of Jesus. She is a model for us, someone to imitate. One old title for Mary is Our Lady, Star of the Sea. Just as stars guide sailors to safety, Mary guides us to her Son.

3. Distribute Activity Sheet 18. Tell the children that we can imitate Mary in three ways. She listened to God, trusted God, and loved God and others. Read the directions. Have the children work in pairs or groups.

4. Let the children report their answers. You might add these ideas:

1) Mary: Mary agreed to be God's mother. She obeyed civil authority by going with Joseph to Bethlehem for the census. She obeyed religious authorities by presenting Jesus in the temple.
Me: I can obey the commandments and listen to my parents and others in authority. I can read God's word in the Bible. I can pray.

2) Mary: She didn't know what being Mother of God would mean. For example, it was risky to be pregnant before marriage. She traveled to Bethlehem while very pregnant. Once, Jesus was missing for three days. Once, neighbors tried to throw Jesus off a cliff. Her Son was criticized and crucified.
Me: I can trust God when I, or someone I love, is sick, or when I'm asked to do something frightening or something goes wrong.

3) Mary: She did what God wanted. She loved Jesus. She went to help Elizabeth. She assisted newlyweds at Cana. She prays for us.
Me: I can learn more about God, pray, read the gospels to learn about Jesus, show love by obeying God, and love my family, friends, and neighbors.

Prayer

Mary, pray that I become more like you so that when I die, Jesus will say, "Come in. You remind me so much of my mother."

Mary, the Best Disciple and Our Model

Mary teaches us how to follow her Son by her example. She always listened to God and obeyed. She trusted God even when things looked impossible or she didn't understand. Mary also loved God and other people. In the first column, write when Mary did these things. In the second column, write how you can imitate her in that way.

MARY	ME
Mary listened to God.	
Mary trusted God.	
Mary loved God and others.	

19 OUR LADY OF LOURDES: HEALTH OF THE SICK

Objective

The children will be familiar with the story of Lourdes and Mary's concern for the sick.

Catechist Notes

From humble beginnings in 1858, Lourdes has become a beloved Catholic pilgrimage spot. The site has four churches, including a large basilica. Healed people leave behind crutches and braces. People who are healthy also come to Lourdes as an act of piety, honoring Our Lady, who shows a mother's care for the sick. Bernadette, Mary's chosen messenger, died of tuberculosis at age thirty-five and was canonized in 1933. At http://en.lourdes-france.org/tv-lourdes/a live video of the sanctuary of Lourdes can be viewed. This website contains much information about Lourdes. You might invite someone who has been to the shrine to speak to your children.

Materials

- ☐ A vial of Lourdes water (optional)
- ☐ Holy cards or a picture of Our Lady of Lourdes
- ☐ Copies of Activity Sheet 19

Activity

1. Ask if the children have ever been very sick. Call on a few to tell how they felt. Comment that Mary has a heart for the sick.

2. Explain the shrine at Lourdes. If possible, show a vial of Lourdes water and pass out holy cards and/or show a picture of Our Lady of Lourdes.
   - In Lourdes, France, there is a sanctuary to Mary that has healing waters. Every year, millions of sick and disabled people travel there in hopes of a cure. Cures are studied in detail by doctors before they are claimed to be miracles. At least sixty-nine healings have been declared miraculous. Many people who are not healed physically experience a new peace.
   - At Lourdes, people go into the water at one of eighteen baths.
   - The sanctuary of Lourdes began in 1858 when Mary appeared to Saint Bernadette, who was only fourteen years old. Bernadette's family of six was so poor that for a few years they lived in an old jail. Bernadette was only four feet and seven inches tall. She was sickly and not very bright. In fact, she used to say, "I'm good for nothing." But Mary chose this unlikely girl to deliver her message.

3. Distribute Activity Sheet 19. Assign parts (Narrator, Bernadette, Reporters 1, 2, 3, 4), choosing a good reader for the role of Saint Bernadette.

4. Describe some of the events in Lourdes today.
   - Every day, except in winter, there are two processions at Lourdes. One is with the Blessed Sacrament, and the other is a candlelight procession at night. At the candlelight procession, the Rosary is prayed and a special Lourdes hymn is sung.

5. Ask what the children could do to help the sick. (visit, send cards, email or phone, etc.)

6. Invite the children to think of sick or disabled people they would like to pray for. Tell them they can say their name aloud in a prayer. Then pray the prayer below.

Prayer

Mary, you care about sick people, especially (names). Please pray that they have patience and peace during their illness—and that they might be healed, if it is God's will.

A Press Conference with Saint Bernadette

NARRATOR: We are pleased to have Saint Bernadette with us to answer your questions about Our Lady of Lourdes.

REPORTER 1: Saint Bernadette, how did you come to see Mary?

BERNADETTE: I was gathering firewood with my sister and a friend. Because of my asthma and weakness, I lagged behind. When I was in front of the grotto, or small cave, I saw a beautiful lady.

REPORTER 2: What did she look like?

BERNADETTE: The lady wore a white robe tied with a blue sash. She had a long white veil. There was a yellow rose on each foot, and she held a rosary with pearl beads and a gold chain. She was about sixteen or seventeen.

REPORTER 3: How many times did you see the lady?

BERNADETTE: Eighteen. But at first my mother, the priests, and city officials thought I was lying or crazy. I was threatened with jail for disturbing the peace because thousands of people came to the grotto to witness the visits.

REPORTER 4: What convinced the doubters that you saw Mary?

BERNADETTE: When I asked her name, she said, "I am the Immaculate Conception." I repeated that to our priest. He knew I didn't know its meaning. The pope had just declared that doctrine. Also, a doctor saw me in a trance, looking at the lady. My candle burned my hand for fifteen minutes, but I wasn't hurt.

REPORTER 1: What did Our Lady want?

BERNADETTE: She told me to have a chapel built at the site where processions could be held. She had me dig in the dirt, and a spring came forth. People who touched the water were healed.

REPORTER 2: What did you talk about?

BERNADETTE: We prayed the Rosary, but she only said the Glory Bes. We spoke about sinners, and she looked sad and said, "Penance. Penance. Penance." Once, she said that I would not have happiness in this life but in the next. I did suffer much before dying young.

REPORTER 3: Didn't seeing Mary and getting attention make you proud?

BERNADETTE: I entered the convent, where I worked in the infirmary. The Sisters kept me from being proud, but I knew that everything was God's doing. I was like a broom. When the sweeping is done, it's put in the corner.

REPORTER 4: Today because of what happened in Lourdes, France, each year six million pilgrims visit and pray at the grotto there. Thank you, St. Bernadette!

20 OUR LADY OF FATIMA: REFUGE OF SINNERS

Objective

The children will heed Mary's messages from her appearances at Fatima.

Catechist Notes

In 1917, Mary appeared at Cova da Iria, in Fatima, Portugal. World War I was raging, and Mary urged prayer and repentance for peace. Both at Lourdes and Fatima, the Blessed Mother appeared to children. This recalls Jesus' teaching that we must become like children to enter the kingdom of heaven. Mary's message is simple enough for children: pray the Rosary and do penance. You might elaborate that Saint John Paul II was bending to see a girl's Fatima badge when an assassin shot. Bullets missed his head. One lodged in his abdomen, just missing a main artery. Hitting it would have killed the pope. Later, the pope visited the would-be assassin in prison and forgave him. Someone who visited Fatima could be a guest speaker. The World Apostolate of Fatima (formerly the Blue Army) offers additional information at www.wafusa.org.

Materials

- ☐ Pictures of the Basilica of Fatima (optional)
- ☐ Copies of Activity Sheet 20

Activity

1. Introduce the apparition of Our Lady of Fatima.
   - In the last century, Mary showed concern for sinners in an extraordinary way. She appeared to three children in Fatima, Portugal, as they were shepherding their flock.
   - Mary's message to them and to the world was to pray for sinners and to do penance. A penance is a prayer or action that shows sorrow for our sins and a willingness to change.
   - Mary also urged them to pray the Rosary. She called herself Our Lady of the Rosary. When we pray the Rosary, we pray fifty-three Hail Marys. In this prayer we ask Mary to pray for us sinners.
2. Distribute Activity Sheet 20. Invite different children to read each section aloud.
3. Tell about modern-day Fatima. If possible, show pictures.
   - Today, about four million pilgrims and tourists visit Fatima each year.
   - The Sanctuary of Fatima includes buildings and structures related to Fatima. One of the main buildings is the Basilica of Our Lady of the Rosary of Fatima, which contains the tombs of Lucia dos Martos and Francisco and Jacinta Marti. Surrounding the basilica are chapels and a hospital.
   - Torchlight processions are held in which a statue of Our Lady of Fatima is carried.
4. During a ceremony consecrating the world to Mary, Pope Francis offered this prayer to Our Lady of Fatima:

   "Guide our lives in your arms. Bless and strengthen every desire for goodness; revive and grow faith; sustain and illuminate hope; arouse and enliven charity; guide all of us on the path of holiness."
   - Read the prayer again slowly.
   - Distribute paper and pens. Invite the children to write their own prayer, asking Our Lady of Fatima to help them grow in faith, hope, love, and holiness.

Prayer

Mary, make me live in God, with God, and for God.

Our Lady of Fatima Timeline

1916: Three times an angel appears to nine-year-old Lucia and her cousins, eight-year-old Francisco and his sister, six-year-old Jacinta. The angel calls himself the angel of peace and teaches them to pray and sacrifice.

MAY 13, 1917: While the children are watching sheep, a lady in light appears over a small oak. She wants them to return on the thirteenth of each month for the next six months. She tells them to pray the Rosary that the war would end. Lucia's mother is angry. She thinks Lucia is lying about the lady.

JUNE 13, 1917: The lady tells the children to pray the Rosary daily and predicts that they will go to heaven. Lucia will live longer to promote devotion to Mary's Immaculate Heart.

JULY 13, 1917: Thousands gather. The lady gives the children a three-part secret. First, the children glimpse hell. The lady says that sinners can be saved by devotion to her and sacrifice. She predicts that if people do not repent, there will be another war. Second, the lady asks that Russia be consecrated to her Immaculate Heart and that people receive Communion on the first Saturday of five consecutive months. The third part was to remain secret.

AUGUST 13, 1917: A city official captures the children on the way to see the lady. He imprisons them for two days and threatens to boil them in oil. The lady came to them on the nineteenth instead.

SEPTEMBER 13, 1917: The lady promised the cure of some people who were sick.

OCTOBER 13, 1917: On a rainy day, Lucia tells the crowd of more than 70,000 people to close their umbrellas. The lady asks that a chapel be built there. She says that God is much offended by sins. After she leaves, the crowd sees the sun whirl in the sky and shoot off rainbow colors. It plunges toward earth and then returns. The children see visions of the mysteries of the Rosary. People find that their previously soaked clothes are now dry.

APRIL 4, 1919: Francisco dies in a flu epidemic. A chapel is being built.

FEBRUARY 29, 1920: Jacinta dies of the flu.

1925: Lucia enters the convent.

MARY 13, 1928: A foundation stone is laid for a basilica in Fatima.

1930: The bishop declares the apparitions worthy of belief. Hundreds of cures have occurred there.

MAY, 13, 1981: Pope Saint John Paul II is shot. He attributes his survival to the Immaculate Heart of Mary and sends the bullet to be placed in the statue of Mary's crown at Fatima.

JUNE 7, 1981: Pope Saint John Paul II and other bishops consecrate the world to the Immaculate Heart of Mary.

2000: Pope Saint John Paul II releases the third part of the secret written by Lucia. Its meaning is unclear. Francisco and Jacinta are declared blessed on May 13.

FEBRUARY 13, 2005: Lucia dies of old age.

21 OUR LADY OF GUADALUPE: PATRONESS OF THE AMERICAS

Objective

The children will know the story of Mary's appearances to Saint Juan Diego in Mexico.

Catechist Notes

The Basilica of Our Lady of Guadalupe is the most visited Catholic shrine. It stands where a shrine to the Aztec mother goddess was. Masses are celebrated continuously before the tilma (cloak) that bears Mary's image. The name Guadalupe is thought to be derived from the Our Lady of Guadalupe shrine in Castile, Spain. St. Juan Diego's surname, Cuauhtlatoatzin, means "the eagle who speaks." In 1999, the church proclaimed Our Lady of Guadalupe the Protectress of the Unborn. The stars and moon in her image echo those in the description of the woman in Revelation. You might invite someone who visited the basilica to be a guest speaker. A video is at http://www.sancta.org/basilica.html.

Materials

- ☐ An image of Our Lady of Guadalupe
- ☐ Pens or pencils
- ☐ Copies of Activity Sheet 21

Activity

1. Invite the children to describe how mothers show love for their children. Then comment:
   - A mother's love for her child runs deep and wide. Just as Mary loved her son, Jesus, so she loves each of us.
   - Mary showed her love when she appeared in Mexico about 500 years ago as Our Lady of Guadalupe. Under this title, Mary is the patroness of the Americas.

2. Distribute Activity Sheet 21. Tell the children that they will learn the story of Our Lady of Guadalupe as they figure out the missing words on the sheet.

3. When the children are finished, call on several to read the story aloud. (**Answers:** *Aztec, Tepeyac, Immaculate, Spanish, sign, uncle, mother, tilma, Basilica, cactus.*)

4. Discuss the story of Our Lady of Guadalupe.
   - How did Mary show herself to be a good mother in her appearances to Saint Juan Diego? (She asked to have a church built where she could hear the prayers of her children. She cured his uncle. She provided roses in December. She left her image on his cloak.)
   - Why do you think Mary appeared to Saint Juan Diego and not the bishop? (She wanted to show love for the Aztec Indians and a poor, humble man.)
   - Artists added gold and silver plating to the image. This has flaked, but the colors of the image itself are like new.

5. Show an image of Our Lady of Guadalupe and explain its symbolism.
   - Mary is in front of the sun and resting her foot on the moon. The sun and moon are symbols of Aztec gods.
   - The stars on Mary's mantle are constellations in the sky on December 12.
   - The blue-green of her mantle is the Aztec color of royalty.
   - The black cross on the pin at her neck was the sign of the Franciscan missionaries to Mexico.
   - Her black belt is the Aztec sign for pregnancy.
   - The four-petal flower over her stomach is a sign of life and deity.

Prayer

Our Lady of Guadalupe, my mother and patroness, whenever I need help, may I turn to you with confidence.

Our Lady of Guadalupe

Use the code to fill in the missing words in the story.

A	B	C	D	E	F	G	H	I	J	K	L	M	N	O	P	Q	R	S	T	U	V	W	X	Y	Z
1	2	3	4	5	6	7	8	9	10	11	12	13	14	15	16	17	18	19	20	21	22	23	24	25	26

Juan Diego was an __________________ **(1-26-20-5-3)** Indian in Mexico. He was on his way to church on December 9, 1531, when he heard birds and saw rainbow colors at __________________**(20-5-16-5-25-1-3)** Hill. A young, pregnant Aztec woman appeared and said she was the ______________________________ **(9-13-13-1-3-21-12-1-20-5)** Virgin Mary. She told Juan to go to the bishop and ask him build a church there. She said, "I am the mother of all. Here I will listen to people's prayers, and I will help them."

Juan Diego went to the _________________ **(19-16-1-14-9-19-8)** bishop but was not believed. Juan Diego suggested that Mary get a better speaker, but she said she had chosen him. Juan went again to the bishop. This time the bishop told him to ask for a ______________ **(19-9-7-14)** that it was really the Mother of God.

Then Mary told Juan that she would give him a sign the next day. But the next day Juan stayed home to care for his deathly ill ________________ **(21-14-3-12-5)**. On the following day, as he went to get a priest, he avoided the hill. But Mary appeared to him anyway, and Juan apologized for not meeting her. Mary scolded, "Do you not know that I am your _____________________ **(13-15-20-8-5-18)**? Are you not under my protection? Your uncle is well already." Then she directed Juan to climb the hill and pick the roses there. Now, it was winter, and nothing grew on the stony hill, but Juan Diego obeyed. He found beautiful roses and brought them to Mary. She bent and arranged them in his ________________ **(20-9-12-13-1)**, or cloak, and told him to take them to the bishop.

When Juan Diego opened his tilma before the bishop, the roses cascaded to the floor. The bishop cried, "The Immaculate!" He knelt and asked Mary's pardon for not believing Juan. Not only were the roses a miracle, but there, imprinted on the tilma, was Mary's image as she appeared to Juan.

A church was built, and Juan Diego lived in a hut beside it, telling people the story of Our Lady of Guadalupe. In the next decade, eight million Aztec Indians became Christian. Today Juan is known as Saint Juan Diego, and millions visit the __________________ **(2-1-19-9-12-9-3-1)** of Guadalupe in Mexico City each year. They view the *tilma* made from ______________ **(3-1-3-20-21-19)** fibers that ordinarily don't last more than thirty years. We celebrate the feast of Our Lady of Guadalupe on December 12.

22 MIRACULOUS MEDAL: HELP OF CHRISTIANS

Objective

The children will understand the meaning of the Miraculous Medal.

Catechist Notes

The Miraculous Medal (Medal of the Immaculate Conception) was entrusted to Sister Catherine Labouré. Children might learn more about this saint, who suffered as Mary predicted. The medal was delayed. The altar and statue Mary asked to be erected were completed only after Catherine's death. You might purchase Miraculous Medals. Autom (autom.com) offers inexpensive ones. The children could cut out the stars on Activity Sheet 22 and attach them to a bulletin board around Mary's picture (or place them before her statue) for the Activity 5 prayer.

Materials

- ☐ A medal, any kind
- ☐ Pens or pencils
- ☐ Copies of Activity Sheet 22

Activity

1. Show a medal and state its purpose. Ask for other examples of medals. (an Olympic medal, a medal for heroism, a commemorative medal)

2. Introduce the Miraculous Medal.
   - Catholics wear the Miraculous Medal in honor of Mary. It shows we are devoted to her.
   - Why do you think it has that name? (It was given miraculously. Miracles come to those who wear it and live the faith.)
   - The medal bears this prayer: "O Mary, conceived without sin, pray for us who have recourse to thee." To have recourse means to turn to someone for help. Mary, our mother, is eager to pray for us when we ask.

3. Tell the story of the Miraculous Medal.
   - Saint Catherine Labouré lived in France. When she was nine, her mother died. Catherine took Mary as her mother. In 1830, Catherine joined the Daughters of Charity. That year, a voice calling her name woke her. A boy said, "The Blessed Virgin awaits you." He led Catherine to the chapel. Mary sat in the priest's chair. Catherine knelt. Mary foretold trouble for France and a mission for Catherine. She was to tell only a priest about her vision. But the priest didn't believe her.
   - Months later, while Catherine prayed in chapel, she saw Mary standing on a snake coiled over a globe. From jewels on Mary's fingers, rays fell onto the globe, but not from all the jewels. The jewels were graces. Jewels with no rays stood for graces not asked for. Around the vision was a prayer. Mary told Catherine to have a medal made like that vision. She said that whoever wore the blessed medal would receive graces and be protected by her.
   - The vision turned to show an *M* with a cross on top. Below were Jesus' heart crowned with thorns and Mary's heart pierced with a sword. Around this design were twelve stars. The priest finally believed Catherine, and the medals were made. Many people who wore them and asked Mary to pray for cures had their prayers answered.

4. Distribute Activity Sheet 22. Have the children write an intention in each star.

5. Pray the prayer below, with the children naming an intention they wrote.

Prayer

O Mary, conceived without sin, pray for us who have recourse to thee. Please pray for . . .

Intentions Brought to Mary

In each star, write the name of a person or a special intention that you would like Mary to pray for.

23 OUR LADY OF THE ROSARY: OUR LADY OF PEACE

Objective

The children will learn how to pray the Rosary.

Catechist Notes

The Rosary is the most popular and most loved Marian devotion. When illiterate people could not pray the one hundred and fifty psalms, they prayed one hundred and fifty Our Fathers on beads. After the Hail Mary was composed, they substituted it. A blessed rosary is a sacramental. You might provide rosaries for the children. You could begin a rosary-making project or hold a contest to see which family creates the most unique rosary. Another possibility is a living rosary in which people represent beads and lead the group in prayer. After their prayer, participants place a flower or a vigil light before an image of Mary.

Materials

- ☐ A rose, real or artificial
- ☐ A rosary
- ☐ Copies of Activity Sheet 23

Activity

1. Say *rosary* and ask what flower is heard in the word. (rose) Show the rose. Comment:
   - A rose is beautiful and fragrant. People give them as a sign of love.
   - Each prayer of the Rosary is like a rose presented to Mary to honor her and show her love.
   - How do you feel when someone praises your mother? (happy, pleased) Jesus is glad when we honor his mother by praying the Rosary.
   - When Mary appeared at Lourdes and Fatima, she asked us to pray the Rosary. She said to pray it for peace. After the United States was attacked in 2001, Saint John Paul II told us to pray the Rosary for peace.
   - One of Mary's titles is Our Lady of Peace.
2. Show a rosary and explain how to pray it.
   - We keep track of prayers on beads. A century is a hundred years. What is a decade? (ten years) The Hail Mary beads are grouped in tens, so we call these groups decades.
   - Rings with ten knobs and bracelets with ten beads, as well as our ten fingers can also be used to pray decades.
   - Praying the Rosary, we do two things at once. While praying the prayers, we think about an event in the life of Jesus or Mary. These are called mysteries. Can you pat your head and rub your stomach? It takes practice. Praying prayers while thinking of mysteries also takes practice.
   - There are four sets of mysteries: joyful, luminous or light, sorrowful, and glorious. They are prayed on different days of the week.
3. Distribute Activity Sheet 23. Read the directions for praying the Rosary.
4. Ask the children to read each set of mysteries and tell why the name of each fits. (joyful mysteries—happy occasions; luminous mysteries—events that shed light on who Jesus is; sorrowful mysteries—about the death of Jesus; glorious mysteries—wonderful events)
5. Pray a decade with the children. Choose a mystery fitting for the church year or the day. Offer the prayers for peace in a part of the world.
6. Encourage the children to suggest to their family that they pray the Rosary together.

Prayer

Mary, Queen of the Rosary, pray for us.

How to Pray the Rosary, the Gospel on Beads

Make the sign of the cross using the crucifix.

Pray the Apostles' Creed on the crucifix.

On the introductory beads: Pray an Our Father, three Hail Marys, and a Glory Be.

For each decade, recall the mystery and pray: an Our Father on the single bead, Hail Marys on the ten beads, the Glory Be.

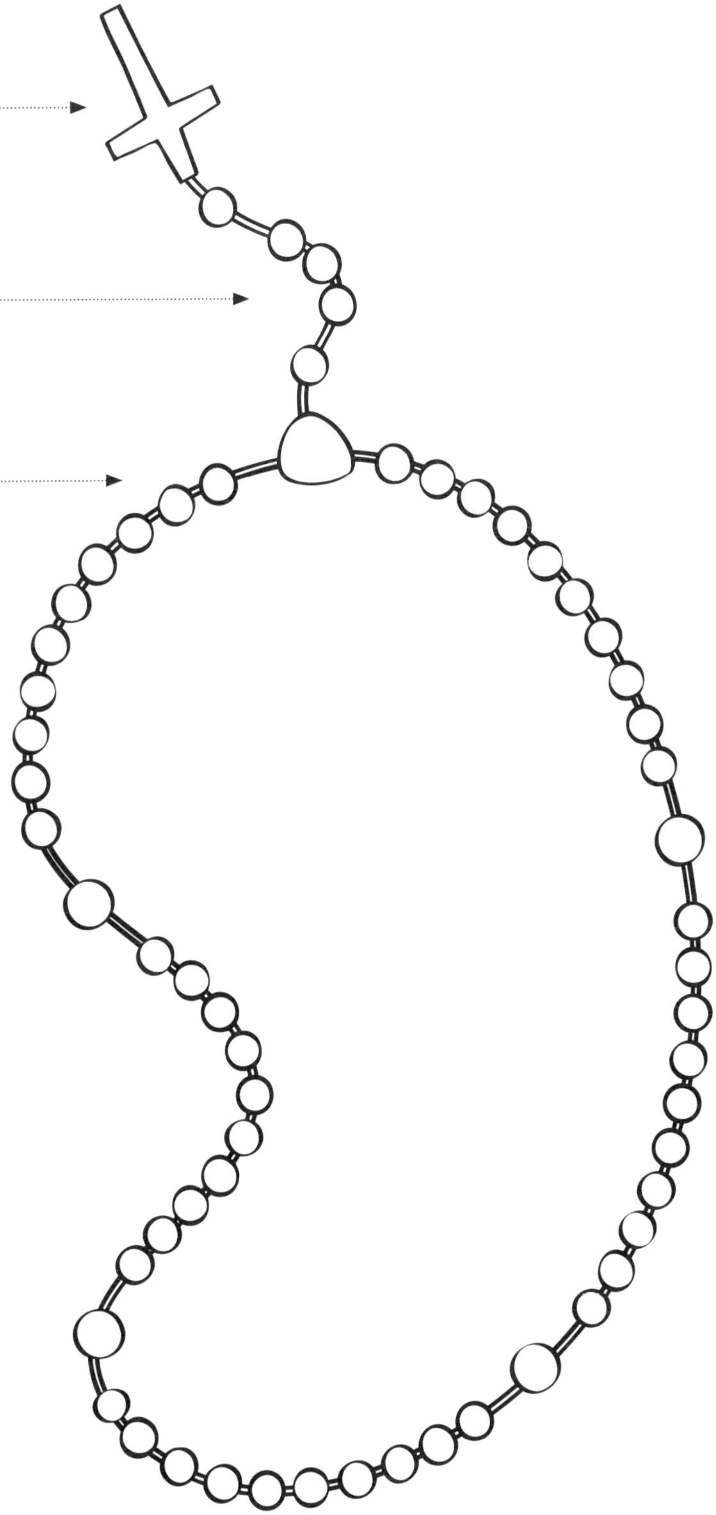

The Joyful Mysteries *(Monday, Saturday)*
1. The Annunciation
2. The Visitation
3. The Birth of Jesus
4. The Presentation in the Temple
5. Finding of the Child Jesus in the Temple

The Luminous Mysteries *(Thursday)*
1. The Baptism in the Jordan River
2. The Wedding at Cana
3. The Proclamation of the Kingdom of God
4. The Transfiguration
5. The Institution of the Eucharist

The Sorrowful Mysteries *(Tuesday, Friday)*
1. The Agony in the Garden
2. The Scourging at the Pillar
3. The Crowning with Thorns
4. The Carrying of the Cross
5. The Crucifixion

The Glorious Mysteries *(Wednesday, Sunday)*
1. The Resurrection
2. The Ascension of Our Lord
3. The Descent of the Holy Spirit
4. The Assumption of Our Lady into Heaven
5. The Coronation of the Blessed Virgin Mary

24 THE SCAPULAR: OUR LADY OF MOUNT CARMEL

Objective

The children will become acquainted with the practice of wearing a scapular.

Catechist Notes

The scapular of Mount Carmel (brown scapular) is the first and most familiar. Others are the blue scapular of the Immaculate Conception and the green scapular of the Immaculate Heart of Mary. Children used to be formally invested in the brown scapular before their First Communion. This is still practiced in some places. You might have your children invested in the scapular. If time permits, tell the story of the contest between the prophet Elijah and the prophets of the false god Baal on Mount Carmel (1 Kings 18:20–39).

Materials

- ☐ A Mount Carmel scapular, cloth or medal
- ☐ A T-shirt with an organization's logo
- ☐ Copies of Activity Sheet 24

Activity

1. Show a T-shirt with an organization's logo. Ask why people wear it. (to show they belong to the organization and support it) Ask children to tell about T-shirts that identify them with a team, organization, or movement.

2. Show a scapular of Mount Carmel and comment:
   - This is the scapular of Mount Carmel, also called the brown scapular.
   - Most brown scapulars have an image of Our Lady of Mount Carmel.
   - People wear this scapular to show love and honor for Mary. They place themselves under her special protection and try to imitate her.
   - Only a priest can bless a scapular and invest a person in it.
   - After someone has been invested, a scapular medal may be worn instead. This has the Sacred Heart of Jesus on one side and Mary on the other.
   - Saint John Paul II, who loved Mary deeply, wore a scapular all his life.

3. Define scapular.
   - *Scapular* comes from the Latin word for shoulder. A habit is clothing that identifies a person as a member of a religious community. Some habits include a scapular, a long, rectangle piece that has a hole for the head and is draped over the shoulders.

4. Tell the story of the scapular's origin.
   - A religious community called Brothers of the Blessed Virgin Mary of Mount Carmel began in Palestine on Mount Carmel. Their patroness was Mary, so they called her Our Lady of Mount Carmel. St. Simon Stock was head of this community in England in the thirteenth century.
   - Mary appeared to Saint Simon. She told him that anyone who wore the Carmelite scapular faithfully would go to heaven. This referred to the Carmelite habit. Later on, the Carmelites made small brown scapulars and gave them to laypeople who belonged to their organizations.
   - The small scapulars became blessed sacramentals. Wearing one symbolizes a person's dedication to God and a willingness to live a good life. The scapular also shows that the person wearing it is devoted to Mary.

5. Distribute Activity Sheet 24. Instruct the children to check the Marian devotions they practice. Encourage them to adopt a new one or two.

Prayer

Mary, may my love for you draw me closer to your Son, Jesus.

Devotion to Mary, Our Lady of Mount Carmel

Those who wear the scapular of Mount Carmel have devotion to Mary and try to imitate her virtues. Put a check before each practice you have. If you have more that are not listed, add them.

- ☐ I pray a Hail Mary every day.
- ☐ I pray three Hail Marys every day.
- ☐ There is an image of Mary in my bedroom.
- ☐ I pray the Rosary.
- ☐ When I'm tempted, I pray to Mary.
- ☐ I try to do what God asks.
- ☐ I do loving deeds for others.
- ☐ I love Jesus.
- ☐ I have holy cards that show Mary.
- ☐ In May, I set up a May altar in honor of Mary.
- ☐ When I need help, I pray to Mary.
- ☐ Besides the Hail Mary, I know another prayer to Mary by heart.
- ☐ I join wholeheartedly in hymns to Mary.
- ☐ I know what is in the gospels about Mary.
- ☐ I pray short prayers to Mary.

☐ Other: ______________________________

25 MARIAN PRAYERS: OUR LADY OF PERPETUAL HELP

Objective

The children will learn more prayers to Mary.

Catechist Notes

St. Francis de Sales said, "Let us run to Mary and, as her little children, cast ourselves into her arms with perfect confidence." At Lourdes, Fatima, and Guadalupe, Mary requested a church be built where she would hear her children's prayers. She told St. Catherine Labouré to have a medal made to encourage us to ask her help. She is truly our mother. You might give each child a holy card of Our Lady of Perpetual Help.

Materials

- ☐ Picture of Our Lady of Perpetual Help
- ☐ Picture of Jean-François Millet's painting "The Angelus" (optional)
- ☐ Scissors
- ☐ Blue construction paper
- ☐ Colored pencils or fine felt-tipped pens
- ☐ Copies of Activity Sheet 25 (three pages)

Activity

1. Show the picture of Our Lady of Perpetual Help.
   - This picture is named for one of Mary's most popular titles, Our Lady of Perpetual Help. What does "perpetual" mean? (neverending, constant)
   - Two angels hold the cross and instruments related to Jesus' death. Looking at the cross, Jesus is frightened but finds comfort in his mother. He ran to Mary so fast that his sandal is falling off. He holds onto her hand.
   - Mary looks at us. She wants us to come to her too when we are in need.

2. Present prayer to Mary.
   - We ask Mary and other saints to pray for us just like we ask friends and relatives to pray for us.
   - We can speak to Mary in our own words, but the church has composed several prayers to her.
   - Set prayers make it easy for us to pray together.

3. Distribute Activity Sheet 25. Introduce each prayer and then pray it with the children.
   - Hail Mary: It is mainly composed of words that the Angel Gabriel and Mary's cousin Elizabeth said to her.
   - *Memorare*: This popular prayer asks Mary's help. (The title, "*Memorare*" is Latin for the first word, "remember.")
   - We Fly to Thy Patronage: This is the oldest known prayer to Mary. It is from about 250 AD. A patron is someone who supports and helps. Mary is our patroness, so we say that we fly to her patronage.
   - Hail, Holy Queen (*Salve Regina* is the Latin translation.): An advocate is someone who pleads for you. This prayer is often prayed at the end of the Rosary.
   - The *Angelus*: It is in honor of the Incarnation—God becoming human. Traditionally, bells were tolled at 6:00 AM, noon, and 6:00 PM, reminding people to pray the *Angelus*. [Show Millet's painting, if possible.]
   - Queen of Heaven (*Regina Coeli,* in the original Latin): This prayer is used in place of the *Angelus* during the Easter season.
   - Short prayers: We can pray little prayers to Mary anytime during the day.

4. Help the children make Marian prayer books from Activity Sheet 25. Encourage using them and memorizing the prayers.

Prayer

O Mary, I love you.

My Marian Prayerbook

Cut apart the prayers into four sections. Fold a piece of blue construction paper in half. Glue the prayers on the pages as indicated. Decorate the pages with Marian symbols: stars, a dove, a lily, a crown, a capital M.

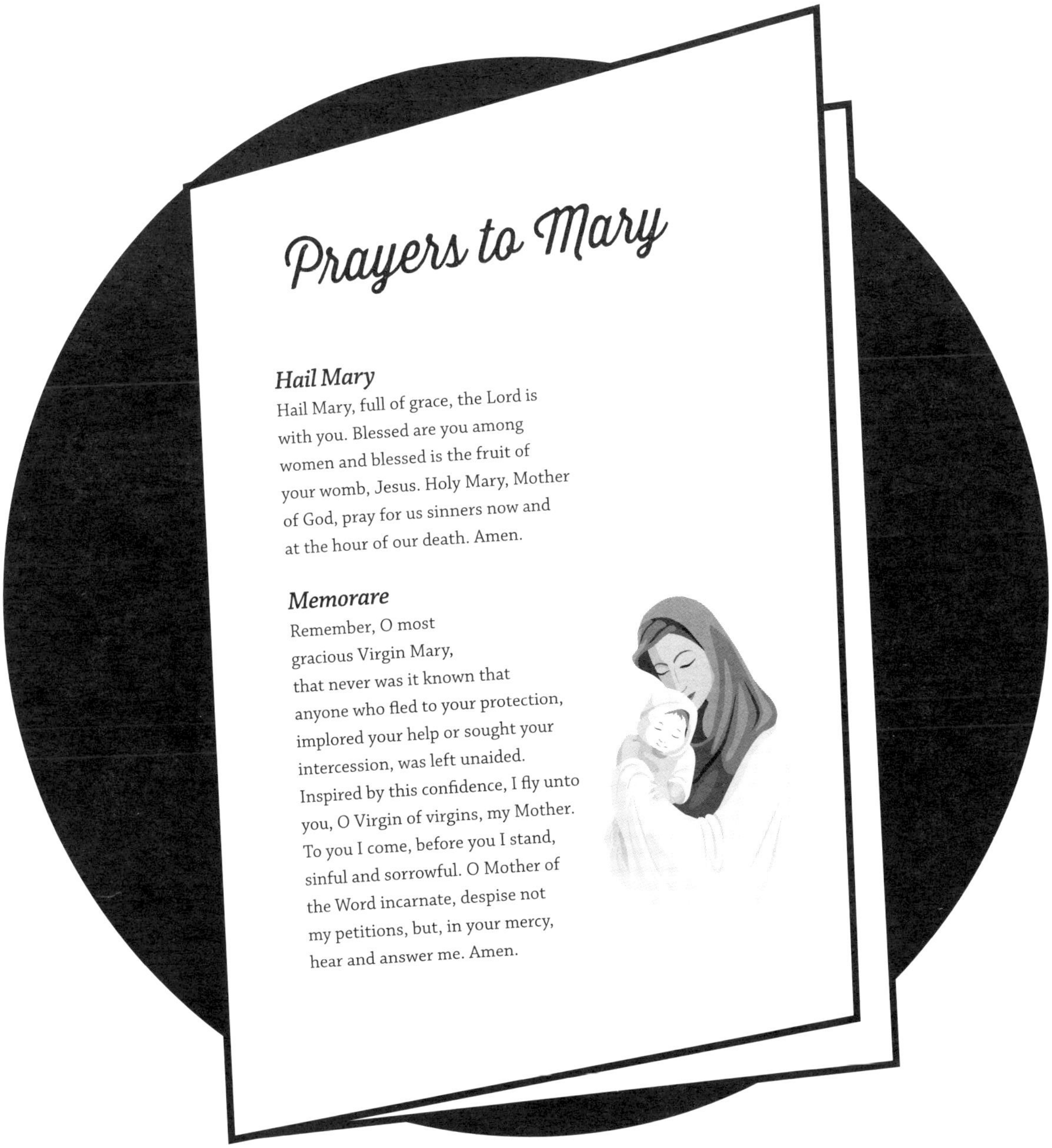

Prayers to Mary

Hail Mary

Hail Mary, full of grace, the Lord is with you. Blessed are you among women and blessed is the fruit of your womb, Jesus. Holy Mary, Mother of God, pray for us sinners now and at the hour of our death. Amen.

Memorare

Remember, O most gracious Virgin Mary, that never was it known that anyone who fled to your protection, implored your help or sought your intercession, was left unaided. Inspired by this confidence, I fly unto you, O Virgin of virgins, my Mother. To you I come, before you I stand, sinful and sorrowful. O Mother of the Word incarnate, despise not my petitions, but, in your mercy, hear and answer me. Amen.

Prayers to Mary

Hail Mary

Hail Mary, full of grace, the Lord is with you. Blessed are you among women and blessed is the fruit of your womb, Jesus. Holy Mary, Mother of God, pray for us sinners now and at the hour of our death. Amen.

Memorare

Remember, O most gracious Virgin Mary, that never was it known that anyone who fled to your protection, implored your help or sought your intercession, was left unaided. Inspired by this confidence, I fly unto you, O Virgin of virgins, my Mother. To you I come, before you I stand, sinful and sorrowful. O Mother of the Word incarnate, despise not my petitions, but, in your mercy, hear and answer me. Amen.

The Angelus

The angel of the Lord declared unto Mary.
And she conceived of the Holy Spirit.
Hail Mary, . . .

Behold the handmaid of the Lord.
Be it done unto me according to Thy word.
Hail Mary, . . .

And the Word was made Flesh.
And dwelt among us.
Hail Mary, . . .

Pray for us, O holy Mother of God.
That we may be made worthy
of the promises of Christ.

Let us pray.
Pour forth, we beseech Thee, O Lord, Thy grace into our hearts, that we to whom the Incarnation of Christ thy Son was made known by the message of an angel, may by his Passion and Cross be brought to the glory of his Resurrection. Through the same Christ Our Lord. Amen.

Queen of Heaven (*Regina Coeli*)

Queen of heaven, rejoice! Alleluia.
The Son whom you mer-
ited to bear, Alleluia,
Has risen as he said, Alleluia.
Pray for us to God, Alleluia.
Rejoice and be glad, O Virgin Mary. Alleluia.
For the Lord has truly risen. Alleluia.

Let us pray.
O God, who, through the resurrection of your Son our Lord Jesus Christ, did vouchsafe to make glad the whole world, grant, we beseech you, that, through his Virgin Mother, Mary, we may obtain the joys of everlasting life. Through the same Christ our Lord. Amen.

Short Prayers

- O Mary conceived without sin,
  pray for us who have recourse to you.
- My Mother, I put my trust in you.
- Mary, Queen of Peace, pray for us.

We Fly to Thy Patronage

We fly to thy patronage, O holy Mother of God;
Despise not our petitions in our necessities,
but deliver us always from all dangers,
O glorious and blessed Virgin. Amen.

Hail, Holy Queen (*Salve Regina*)

Hail, holy Queen, Mother of mercy, our life, our sweetness and our hope. To thee do we cry, poor banished children of Eve. To thee do we send up our sighs, mourning and weeping in this valley of tears. Turn then, most gracious Advocate, thine eyes of mercy toward us, and after this our exile, show unto us the blessed fruit of thy womb, Jesus.

O clement, O loving, O sweet Virgin Mary!
Pray for us, O Holy Mother of God,
That we may be made worthy of
the promises of Christ. Amen.

26 LITANY OF MARY: MYSTICAL ROSE

Objective

The children will become familiar with the Litany of Loreto and the meaning of some of Mary's titles.

Catechist Notes

The Litany of Loreto was approved in 1587 by Pope Sixtus V. It has been set to music by Mozart and other composers. Saint John Paul II added these invocations to it: Mother of the Church (added in 1980) and Queen of Families (added in 1995).

Materials

- ☐ WORDS ON THE BOARD OR ON FLASHCARDS: *CHASTE, INVIOLATE, UNDEFILED, AMIABLE, COUNSEL, PRUDENT, VENERABLE, VESSEL, AFFLICTED*
- ☐ DRAWING PAPER
- ☐ CRAYONS, PAINTS, OR FELT-TIPPED PENS
- ☐ COPIES OF ACTIVITY SHEET 26

Activity

1. Introduce the concept of titles in a litany.
   - We honor certain people by giving them titles. A great basketball player might be dubbed "King of the Courts." An outstanding cook might be called "Queen of the Kitchen." Can you think of other titles like this?
   - A litany is a prayer that addresses someone by a number of titles or qualities. After each one is mentioned, a response is repeated.
   - The Litany of the Blessed Virgin Mary was composed during the Middle Ages. It is also called the Litany of Loreto because it was prayed at the shrine of the Holy House at Loreto, Italy. The house is supposedly where Mary lived. Many believe it was carried to Loreto by angels.
   - The many titles in the litany help us reflect on Mary's privileges, holiness, power, and majesty.
2. Show the flashcards and define these words in the Litany of Loreto:
   - *Chaste* means pure.
   - *Inviolate* and *undefiled* mean without sin.
   - *Amiable* means pleasant, friendly, warmhearted.
   - *Counsel* means advice.
   - *Prudent* means having good judgment.
   - *Venerable* means worthy of great respect.
   - A *vessel* is a container.
   - The *afflicted* means those who are suffering.
3. Explain three of the titles in the Litany of Loreto.
   - We call Mary "mystical rose" because she is lovely like this beautiful flower. *Mystical* means spiritual.
   - The "ark of the covenant" was a chest that God had Moses make. Within this ark, God was present with his people. Mary is like this ark because she carried God within her.
   - The "morning star" is the planet Venus, which shines right before sunrise. Mary is the bright light that heralded the coming of Jesus.
4. Pray the Litany of Loreto with the children. Instruct them to read the parts in italics.
5. Direct the children to choose a title of Mary from the litany and illustrate it. Then let them tell about their drawings.

Prayer

"Dearest Mother,...bless us in your heart, comfort us in our pains, stand by us in all distress, show us Jesus after our death." » HILDEGARD OF BINGEN

Litany of Loreto

Lord, have mercy.

Christ, have mercy.

Lord, have mercy. Christ, hear us.

Christ, graciously hear us.

God, the Father of heaven,
have mercy on us.

God, the Son, Redeemer of the world,
have mercy on us.

God, the Holy Spirit,
have mercy on us.

Holy Trinity, One God,
have mercy on us.

RESPONSE: *pray for us.*

Holy Mary,
Holy Mother of God,
Holy Virgin of virgins,
Mother of Christ,
Mother of divine grace,
Mother most pure,
Mother most chaste,
Mother inviolate,
Mother undefiled,
Mother most amiable,
Mother most admirable,
Mother of good counsel,
Mother of our Creator,
Mother of our Savior,
Mother of the Church,
Virgin most prudent,
Virgin most venerable,
Virgin most renowned,
Virgin most powerful,
Virgin most merciful,
Virgin most faithful,
Mirror of justice,
Seat of wisdom,
Cause of our joy,
Spiritual vessel,
Vessel of honor,
Singular vessel of devotion,
Mystical rose,
Tower of David,
Tower of ivory,
House of gold,
Ark of the covenant,
Gate of heaven,
Morning star,
Health of the sick,
Refuge of sinners,
Comforter of the afflicted,
Help of Christians,
Queen of angels,
Queen of patriarchs,
Queen of prophets,
Queen of apostles,
Queen of martyrs,
Queen of confessors,
Queen of virgins,
Queen of all saints,
Queen conceived without original sin,
Queen assumed into heaven,
Queen of the most holy Rosary,
Queen of families,
Queen of peace.

Lamb of God, who take away the sins of the world,
Spare us, O Lord.

Lamb of God, who take away the sins of the world,
Graciously hear us, O Lord.

Lamb of God, who take away the sins of the world.
Have mercy on us.

Pray for us, O holy Mother of God,
That we may be made worthy of the promises of Christ.

Let us pray. Grant, we beg you, O Lord God, that we your servants, may enjoy lasting health of mind and body, and by the glorious intercession of the Blessed Mary, ever Virgin, be delivered from present sorrow and enter into the joy of eternal happiness. Through Christ our Lord.

Amen.

27 OLD TESTAMENT TYPES OF MARY: THE NEW EVE

Objective

The children will identify people and items in the Old Testament that prefigure Mary.

Catechist Notes

In salvation history, some Old Testament events and people resemble those in the New Testament. In the Letter to the Romans, for instance, Adam, the first man, is viewed as a type of Christ, the new man. Patterns found in the Old Testament come to full revelation in the New Testament. Making connections between types and antitypes is called "typology," a way to interpret the Bible. The opening activity can be made more interesting by having the children name objects that you show by casting their shadows from behind a sheet lit by a flashlight.

Materials

- ☐ Flashlight (optional)
- ☐ Sheet (optional)
- ☐ Pens or pencils
- ☐ Copies of Activity Sheet 27

Activity

1. Cast a shadow of your hand using natural light, lights, or a flashlight. Point out that the shadow has the shape of the real image. The two are alike. The shadow reveals what the object is like.

2. Explain types and figures.
   - Some people, events, and objects in the Old Testament foreshadow what is in the New Testament. We call them types or figures. They give us clues of, they prefigure, what is to come.
   - For example, Noah's ark, which saved people, prefigured the church, which saves people. Jonah, who was in a large fish for three days, prefigures Jesus, who was in the tomb for three days.

3. Name Old Testament types and ask what they are like in the New Testament.
   - Isaac carries the wood on which he is to be sacrificed up a mountain. (Jesus carried the cross up Calvary.)
   - Joseph forgave his brothers for selling him. (Jesus forgives us, his brothers and sisters.)
   - The Israelites' firstborn sons were saved by the blood of a lamb on their doors. (The blood of Jesus saved us.)
   - The Israelites were freed from slavery in Egypt by passing through the Red Sea. (We are freed from sin and Satan by the waters of baptism.)
   - God provided manna, bread from heaven, for the Israelites. (Jesus gave us the Eucharist.)
   - Moses was a prophet and leader who gave the Israelites the law. (Jesus is the new Moses who gave us a new commandment.)
   - Moses held up a bronze serpent on a pole, and sick people who looked up at it were cured. (Jesus on the cross saved us.)

4. Comment that some Old Testament types prefigure Our Lady. Distribute Activity Sheet 27. Tell the children to match the types in the first column with what they prefigure in the second.

5. When the children are finished, check their work. **Answers:** *1) D; 2) F; 3) A; 4) H; 5) C; 6) I; 7) G; 8) E; 9) B.*

6. Introduce the prayer below by explaining that after Judith slew the enemy, her people praised her with words we now use for Mary.

Prayer

"You are the glory of Jerusalem, you are the great boast of Israel, you are the great pride of our nation!" » JUDITH 15:9

Types That Prefigure the Blessed Virgin Mary

For each type in Column 1, find what it best prefigures in Column 2 and write its letter on the line.

COLUMN 1	COLUMN 2
① ___ **Jacob's ladder.** In a dream Jacob saw a ladder that connected earth to heaven.	**A.** Mary is not tainted by sin.
② ___ **Burning bush.** Moses saw a bush on fire that was not consumed. God spoke from it.	**B.** Through Mary we are protected from sin and death.
③ ___ **Manna.** The Israelites ate manna in the desert. Leftover manna that was set aside did not spoil.	**C.** Mary was the temple of God.
④ ___ **Fleece of Gideon.** The fleece was soaked with dew while the ground around it was dry.	**D.** Mary brought God down into the world and enabled us to go up to heaven.
⑤ ___ **Ark of the covenant.** God was present to the people in this chest. It was kept in the Temple.	**E.** Mary intercedes for us.
⑥ ___ **Eve.** Eve is the mother of all human beings.	**F.** Mary carried God within her.
⑦ ___ **Sarah and Hannah.** These women were barren but miraculously gave birth to sons. Abraham's wife Sarah had Isaac, and Hannah had Samuel, who was a prophet and judge.	**G.** Mary's pregnancy was miraculous because she was a virgin.
⑧ ___ **Esther.** This lovely queen risked her life by appearing before the foreign king to beg that the Jewish people not be slaughtered as planned.	**H.** Mary is full of grace.
⑨ ___ **Judith.** When the Israelites were being attacked, this beautiful woman went into the enemy camp and slew the enemy general.	**I.** Mary is the spiritual mother of all people.

28 MARIAN FEAST DAYS

Objective

The children will learn days we celebrate Mary.

Catechist Notes

The church declares Marian feasts and decides whether they will be local, regional, or universal and their degree of celebration (solemnity, feast, memorial, or optional memorial). For older children, introduce the terms *latria* (adoration given to God), *hyperdulia* (reverence paid to Mary), and *dulia* (reverence of the saints). Consider celebrating a feast by a prayer service with the feast's theme. The children might research other Marian feasts.

Materials

- ☐ Pens or pencils
- ☐ Copies of Activity Sheet 28

Activity

1. Discuss days that honor people.
   - We set aside certain days to honor special people. In November, for example, we celebrate Veterans' Day. Who do we remember on that day? (men and women who have fought for our country)
   - What other days do we observe to honor a person or a group? (Mother's Day, Father's Day, Presidents Day, Martin Luther King Day, Secretaries Day)

2. Explain feast days.
   - The church has dedicated days for saints. On those days, called feast days, Mass is celebrated in their honor. Who are some popular saints who have feast days? (Patrick, Joseph, Nicholas, etc.)
   - St. Mary has the most feast days—days on which we honor her and show her our love. Some are celebrated by the church all over the world, while others are celebrated by a certain country.

3. Clarify that we do not worship Mary.
   - Mary is not a goddess but a human being. We do not worship her. Only God is adored and worshipped.
   - We honor and venerate, or reverence, Mary because she is the Mother of God.
   - We also honor and venerate the other saints.

4. Distribute Activity Sheet 28. Explain two feasts the children may be unfamiliar with, and comment on the sentence at the bottom of the sheet:
   - Our Lady of the Snows celebrates the basilica of Saint Mary Major in Rome.
   - The Presentation is based on a story that is not in the Bible. In it, three-year-old Mary is taken to live in the temple and is dedicated to God.
   - On Saturday, the church has Masses in honor of Mary and special prayers to her.
   - May, a lovely spring month, is dedicated to her. So is October, when a battle was won after people prayed the Rosary.

5. Direct the children to mark what each Marian feast celebrates. When they are finished, check their answers. **Answers:** *1) A; 2) E; 3) C; 4) E; 5) C; 6) E; 7) C or D; 8) C; 9) A or E; 10) E; 11) B; 12) E; 13) D or E; 14) D; 15) E; 16) A or B; 17) C.*

6. Ask the children how they could honor Mary on her days. (Pray extra to her. Set her image in a special place. Put flowers before her image. Meditate on a Scripture passage about Mary.)

Prayer

I am all yours, O Jesus, and all I have is yours, through Mary, your most holy mother.

Feast Days in Honor of Mary

Here are the main Marian feast days. Holy days of obligation when we are required to celebrate the Eucharist are in boldface. Mark what each day celebrates, using the code:
A = A doctrine concerning Mary ; **B** = A quality or virtue of Mary
C = An apparition, **D** = A Marian devotion, **E** = An event in Mary's life

1. **JANUARY 1**
   Solemnity of Mary, Mother of God

2. **FEBRUARY 2**
   Presentation of the Lord (Purification of Mary)

3. **FEBRUARY 11**
   Our Lady of Lourdes

4. **MARCH 25**
   Annunciation of the Lord

5. **MAY 13**
   Our Lady of Fatima

6. **MAY 31**
   Visitation

7. **JULY 16**
   Our Lady of Mount Carmel

8. **AUGUST 5**
   Our Lady of the Snows

9. **AUGUST 15**
   Assumption

10. **AUGUST 22**
    Queenship of Mary

11. **SEPTEMBER 12**
    Most Holy Name of Mary

12. **SEPTEMBER 8**
    Birth of Mary

13. **SEPTEMBER 15**
    Our Lady of Sorrows

14. **OCTOBER 7**
    Our Lady of the Rosary

15. **NOVEMBER 21**
    Presentation of the Blessed Virgin Mary

16. **DECEMBER 8**
    Immaculate Conception

17. **DECEMBER 12**
    Our Lady of Guadalupe

Saturday and the months of May and October are dedicated to Mary.

29 MARIAN DEVOTIONS AND HYMNS

Objective

The children will learn about a few Marian devotions and analyze a hymn for truths about her.

Catechist Notes

Devotion to Mary flourished after the Council of Ephesus declared her the Mother of God. It surged in the Middle Ages, though it was sometimes characterized by excess. The Second Vatican Council and the *Catechism of the Catholic Church* recommend Marian devotions. As Reverend William Joseph Chaminade noted, "We go to God through Mary, as faith tells us he came to us through her." Fuller explanations of the Miraculous Medal, the Rosary, and scapulars are in lessons 22, 23, and 24 respectively. Also, a May crowning is carried out in lesson 16. You might take the children on a pilgrimage to an image of Mary, or several of them, on your church property and pray a decade of the Rosary at each. They might do research to discover more about Mary's flowers.

Materials

- ☐ A recording of a Marian hymn such as "Ave Maria" or "Immaculate Mary"
- ☐ Equipment to play a recording
- ☐ Pens or pencils
- ☐ Drawing paper
- ☐ Crayons or felt-tipped pens
- ☐ Copies of Activity Sheet 29

Activity

1. Introduce devotions.
   - What is your favorite color?
   - Artists often present Mary wearing blue. The color blue was a royal color worn by an empress. It also stands for purity. People sometimes wear something blue in honor of Mary. This is a way to show their love and devotion to her.
   - The church honors Mary as the greatest of all the saints. We show our love for Mary through devotions such as praying the Rosary or asking for her intercession.
   - We don't worship Mary but turn to her for her intercession, asking for her prayers on our behalf.
   - All devotions, whether focused on Mary or the saints, lead us to Christ and help us to recognize God's saving grace in our lives.
2. Point out that hymns dedicated to Mary are a form of Marian devotion. Play a recording of a Marian hymn and ask the children how the words reflect Mary's holiness.
3. Distribute Activity Sheet 29. Tell the children to match the devotions with their descriptions. Check their work. **Answers:** *1) C; 2) E; 3) H; 4) A; 5) G; 6) B; 7) J; 8) D; 9) F; 10) I.*
4. Explain Mary gardens.
   - The Basilica of the Immaculate Conception in Washington, DC, has a Mary garden, and so do many parishes.
   - Some flowers related to Mary found in a Mary garden are the rose with thorns (for Mary's beauty and role in salvation), the lily (Mary's purity and holiness), deep-blue iris (Mary's fidelity), gladiolas with sword-shaped leaves (Mary's sorrows), Marigold (named for Mary and symbol of her simplicity and sorrow), blue Columbine (Our Lady's slipper, said to have sprung up where she walked), and the cornflower (Mary's crown).
5. Call on children to read the seven sorrows and seven joys of Mary. Ask for volunteers to draw each one. Display the children's work.

Prayer

"O Lady, by the love that you bear Jesus, help me to love him." » St. Bridget

Devotions to Our Lady

Match each devotion to its description and write the description's letter on the line.

1. ____ **Rosary**
2. ____ **Scapular**
3. ____ **Nine Saturdays**
4. ____ **Miraculous Medal**
5. ____ **May altar**
6. ____ **May crowning**
7. ____ **Pilgrimage**
8. ____ **Traveling statue**
9. ____ **Garden**
10. ____ **Mary candle**

A. A medal of Mary with the prayer "O Mary, conceived without sin, pray for us who have recourse to you."

B. A ritual with a procession, songs, and prayers, during which a statue of Mary is crowned

C. A circle of beads on which prayers are said while mysteries are pondered

D. An image of Mary, such as Our Lady of Fatima, that goes from family to family. Each family prays to her

E. Two small rectangles of cloth draped over the shoulders worn in honor of Mary

F. Flowers named for Mary or related to her life

G. A table or shelf with an image of Mary and decorated with such things as flowers and a candle

H. Receiving Holy Communion nine Saturdays in a row

I. A candle inscribed with an "M" and decorated with blue that is lit on her feasts

J. A journey to a shrine or church dedicated to Mary

Seven Sorrows of Mary

1. The prophecy of Simeon
2. The flight into Egypt
3. The loss of the Child Jesus in the Temple
4. Mary meeting Jesus as he carried his cross
5. The crucifixion
6. Mary receiving the body of Jesus from the cross
7. Jesus' body being placed in the tomb

Seven Joys of Mary

1. The annunciation
2. The nativity of Jesus
3. The adoration of the Magi
4. The resurrection of Christ
5. The ascension of Christ
6. The descent of the Holy Spirit upon the apostles and Mary
7. The coronation of Mary

30 THE BLESSED VIRGIN MARY IN ART

Objective

The children will become acquainted with some famous Marian art.

Catechist Notes

Marian art is diverse in style, medium, and subject. Renaissance artists especially are known for depicting events in Mary's life. Art was an effective way to educate people. For example, in some paintings, Mary enfolds many people under a large mantle to show that she is our protector. You might invite the children to bring statues and pictures of Mary from home.

Materials

- ☐ Statues and pictures of Mary, perhaps as a PowerPoint presentation
- ☐ Pens or pencils
- ☐ Copies of Activity Sheet 30

Activity

1. Ask the children to describe images of Mary they have (or to show them if they brought them).

2. Tell about Mary in art.
   - Mary is a popular figure in art. One of the earliest pictures of her appears in an underground burial place in Rome called a catacomb.
   - Because Jewish people did not make images for fear that they would be worshiped as idols, we do not know what Mary looked like.
   - People in different countries make her like themselves. Our Lady of Guadalupe appeared as an Aztec Indian.
   - Some countries are devoted to Mary as represented by a certain image. In Lithuania, for example, they honor Our Lady of Siluva.
   - Images of Mary may have stars because that is how she appears in the Book of Revelation. Some art shows her immaculate heart.

3. Present and explain images of Mary. Ask which image the children like best and why. If possible include these:
   - Michelangelo's *Pietà*—This statue of Mary holding the crucified Jesus is in the Basilica of St. Peter in Rome.
   - Fra Angelico's *Annunciation*—This is perhaps the most famous of Fra Angelico's paintings.
   - Our Lady of Lourdes—This is based on St. Bernadette's description of Mary, but she said that Our Lady was much more beautiful.
   - Our Lady Untier of Knots—Years ago, Pope Francis brought a copy of this painting home to Argentina from Germany, where he studied. He says Mary "lovingly brings us to God" so he can undo the knots of disobedience in our souls. Mary can also help us solve our knotty problems. In the painting, a ribbon and a serpent are knotted.
   - The *Sistine Madonna*—Paintings of Mary are called Madonnas. The painter Raphael created many of them, but this is the most famous.
   - Our Lady of Częstochowa—This Black Madonna is an icon revered by the Polish people. A legend has it that St. Luke painted this image. It is in the style of "one who shows the way" in that Mary points to Jesus. An icon is symbolic art painted with prayer and fasting.

4. Distribute Activity Sheet 30. Ask the children if they can find the letters *M, A, R,* and *I* in the monogram for Maria. Direct them to write poems about Mary and share them aloud.

Prayer

Mary, make me live in God, with God, and for God.

Pen Picture of Our Blessed Mother

Paint a picture of Mary with words. On the lines below, write a diamante about her. A diamante is a diamond-shaped, seven-line poem. It is a fitting form for Mary because a diamond is precious and so is she.

DIRECTIONS FOR A DIAMANTE

One noun, the topic	Jesus
Two adjectives about the noun	Gentle, humble
Three verbs ending in "-ing"	Loving, forgiving, saving
Four nouns about the topic	Son of God, Nazarene, carpenter, Messiah
Three verbs	Preach, heal, suffer
Two adjectives	Merciful, powerful
A synonym for the topic	King

31 PEOPLE, PLACES, AND THINGS NAMED FOR MARY

Objective

The children will see how love for Mary has been shown by naming people and things for her.

Catechist Notes

More women in the United States have the name Mary or some form of it than any other name. New buildings and institutions are still being named after Mary. In Hebrew, Mary's name is Miryam. Ahead of time, prepare a list of places and buildings in your diocese that are named for our Blessed Mother so you can mention them to the children.

Materials

- ☐ Pens or pencils
- ☐ Small prize (optional)
- ☐ Copies of Activity Sheet 31

Activity

1. Ask the children if they were named for someone, and if so, who. Comment that many women are named for Mary, and in some countries men are too.

2. State that we honor people by naming things for them, such as streets, buildings, or discoveries they made. Offer examples and then ask the children for others:
   - America was named for Amerigo Vespucci, whom some people mistakenly thought had discovered the new world.
   - Rockefeller Center in New York is named for John D. Rockefeller Jr., who leased and developed the site.
   - Chicago's O'Hare Airport is named for Edward O'Hare, a World War II hero.
   - Barnard's Star is named after E.E. Barnard, who discovered it.

3. Distribute copies of Activity Sheet 31. Hold a contest to see who can list the most names that are forms of Mary. In the box, write names that are forms of Mary. After a few minutes, determine the winner and award a prize if you wish. Inform the children of Marian names that they probably did not list: Madonna, Molly, Assumpta, Immaculata, Concepción, Guadalupe, and Dolores, which is derived for *dolor,* Latin for "sorrow."

4. Give examples of places and things named after Mary out of love for her. Include those in your diocese.
   - The flagship of Christopher Columbus's three ships was the Santa Maria, which means Holy Mary.
   - Los Angeles is named for Our Lady of the Angels.
   - Asunción is the capital of Paraguay. It refers to the Assumption of Mary.
   - Fr. Jacques Marquette, SJ, who explored the Mississippi River, named it River of the Immaculate Conception.
   - Notre Dame Cathedral and the University of Notre Dame are named for Mary. *Notre Dame* means "Our Lady."
   - Many churches and schools are named for Mary. So are religious communities such as the Marianists, the Marists, and the Sisters of Notre Dame.

5. Tell the children that we honor Mary by celebrating the Holy Name of Mary on September 12. Stress that the best way to honor Mary is to imitate her by living as God wishes.

6. Direct the children to compose a prayer to Mary on Activity Sheet 31. Invite them to share their prayers with the class.

Prayer

O Mary, you entered the world without stain; obtain for me from God, that I may leave it without sin.

My Prayer to Mary

How many names can you think of that are forms of Mary? List them below:

Compose a prayer to Mary.
Write a line beginning with each letter below.

M ____________________

O ____________________

T ____________________

H ____________________

E ____________________

R ____________________

M ____________________

A ____________________

R ____________________

Y ____________________

32 CHURCHES DEDICATED TO MARY

Objective

The children will learn about notable churches dedicated to the Mother of God.

Catechist Notes

The first Marian shrine to be established in the United States is in St. Augustine, Florida. It is devoted to Our Lady of La Leche (the Milk) and a Happy Delivery. A field trip to a Marian shrine would be a memorable experience for the children. For a list of Marian shrines according to state, go to http://campus.udayton.edu/mary/resources/shrines/us.html. Children may report on a shrine.

Materials

- ☐ Images of one or more Marian basilicas
- ☐ Recordings of two Marian hymns (suggestion: "Mary the Dawn," found on YouTube)
- ☐ Equipment to play recordings
- ☐ Bible
- ☐ Copies of Activity Sheet 32

Activity

1. Tell the children that in the years between 1140 and 1280, about eighty cathedrals, or large churches, in honor of Mary were built in France alone. Ask what churches in your diocese are named for Mary. Mention omitted ones.

2. Present Marian churches, showing images.
   - The Basilica of Mary Major in Rome is one of four great basilicas there. This fourth-century church is also called the Church of Our Lady of the Snows because of a legend. Supposedly, a wealthy couple wanted to donate their goods to the church. On August 4, the couple and the pope all dreamed that Mary told them to build a basilica where it snowed. The next morning snow fell on Esquiline Hill. The basilica's feast day is August 5. During Mass that day, white rose petals are strewn from the dome of the basilica.
   - The Basilica of the Immaculate Conception in Washington, D.C., is in honor of Mary, patroness of the United States. It is the largest Roman Catholic church in North America. It has more than seventy chapels and oratories dedicated to Mary under different titles and as she is venerated in different countries. A huge mosaic, Christ in Majesty, dominates the church.
   - The Basilica of Our Lady of Guadalupe in Mexico houses St. Juan Diego's cloak on which Mary's image appeared.
   - The Basilica of Our Lady of Fatima in Portugal commemorates her visit to three shepherd children.
   - The Basilica of Our Lady of Lourdes in France commemorates her appearance to St. Bernadette. There, people bathe in healing waters, hoping for a cure.

3. State that shrines in honor of Our Lady are located all over the world. Mention any near you.

4. Distribute Activity Sheet 32. Choose a leader and a reader. Designate sides 1 and 2. Explain two of the prayers as below and then carry out the prayer service.
   - Blessed Mother Teresa of Calcutta said, "No Mary. No Jesus." During the prayer service we will pray a very old poem that uses figures of speech to convey that Mary gave birth to Jesus.
   - We will also pray an Act of Consecration to Mary. To consecrate something means to set it aside for God. Consecrating ourselves to Mary means entrusting ourselves to her. We are really dedicating ourselves to her Son through her hands.

Prayer

Sweet heart of Mary, be my salvation.

A Prayer Service to Honor Mary

LEADER: Mary, you were the temple that housed Jesus the Son of God for nine months. Even before that you were full of grace, God's life. Today we honor you and celebrate your privileges. Pray that we too may bear Jesus in our hearts and bring him into our world.

Song

SIDE 1: Mary the dawn,
SIDE 2: Christ the perfect day;

SIDE 1: Mary the gate,
SIDE 2: Christ the heavenly way!

SIDE 1: Mary the root,
SIDE 2: Christ the mystic vine;

SIDE 1: Mary the grape,
SIDE 2: Christ the sacred wine!

SIDE 1: Mary the wheat-sheaf,
SIDE 2: Christ the living bread;

SIDE 1: Mary the rose-tree,
SIDE 2: Christ the rose blood-red!

SIDE 1: Mary the font,
SIDE 2: Christ the cleansing flood;

SIDE 1: Mary the chalice,
SIDE 2: Christ the saving blood!

SIDE 1: Mary the temple,
SIDE 2: Christ the temple's Lord;

SIDE 1: Mary the shrine,
SIDE 2: Christ the God adored!

SIDE 1: Mary the beacon,
SIDE 2: Christ the haven's rest;

SIDE 1: Mary the mirror,
SIDE 2: Christ the vision blest!

SIDE 1: Mary the mother,
SIDE 2: Christ the mother's son.

ALL: Both ever blest while endless ages run. Amen.

Scripture Reading Luke 1:26–38

Silent Reflection

Act of Consecration

ALL:
My Queen and my Mother,
I give myself entirely to you;
and to show my devotion to you,
I consecrate to you this day my eyes,
my ears, my mouth,
my heart, my whole being without reserve.
Wherefore, good Mother,
as I am your own,
keep me, guard me, as your property
and possession. Amen.

Song

OTHER TITLES IN THIS SERIES

Enriching Faith

LESSONS AND ACTIVITIES ON THE BIBLE

Mary Kathleen Glavich, SND

Here are creative ways to introduce biblical lands and cultures, versions of the Bible, biblical reference tools, and techniques for using Scripture as a basis for prayer. Essential topical background, additional teaching ideas, and fun reproducible activity sheets make this a must-have resource, perfect for helping students in grades four and up develop a lifelong understanding and love for sacred Scripture.

72 PAGES | $14.95 | 9781627850278

Enriching Faith

PRAYERS AND ACTIVITIES ON SERVICE

Patricia Mathson

Help children make Christian service a way of life with this creative collection of outreach projects, hands-on learning experiences, and joyful prayers. Each activity speaks to children's hearts and includes easy instructions, curriculum connections, and more. Perfect for parish, school, or home-based programs, and anyone who wants to help children become caring and compassionate followers of Christ.

72 PAGES | $14.95 | 9781585959372

Enriching Faith

LESSONS AND ACTIVITIES ON PRAYER

Catherine Stewart

Here are dozens of fresh ideas to help your students see prayer in a whole new light. Easy-to-do activities like the bouncing Prayer Ball, Gratitude Grab Bags, and Spoons of Thankfulness can help you teach traditional, spontaneous, creative, and even meditative prayer. Complete with directions, templates, discussion starters, parent letters, catechetical information, and much more.

72 PAGES | $14.95 | 9781585959471

Enriching Faith

LESSONS AND ACTIVITIES ON THE TEACHINGS OF JESUS

Lee Danesco

Use this creative and engaging activity book to help you teach children in the first grade and beyond about Jesus' teachings on loving God and neighbor. The activities, reproducible and prayers cover everything from the Sermon on the Mount and the Beatitudes to the Golden Rule and the Our Father. A thorough and practical activity book for every classroom!

72 PAGES | $14.95 | 9781627851046

TO ORDER CALL 1-800-321-0411
OR VISIT WWW.TWENTYTHIRDPUBLICATIONS.COM

TWENTY-THIRD PUBLICATIONS
A division of Bayard, Inc.